The
MAILBOX®
The Education Center®

Phonics Word Study

Grades 2–3

THE BEST OF TEACHER'S HELPER® Magazine

The best reproducible activities from the 2005–2008 issues of *Teacher's Helper®* magazine

- Short and long vowels
- Word families
- Blends and digraphs
- *R*-controlled vowels
- Compound words
- Contractions
- Spelling

And more!

Managing Editor: Hope Taylor Spencer

Editorial Team: Becky S. Andrews, Diane Badden, Kimberley Bruck, Karen A. Brudnak, Pam Crane, Georgia Davis, Lynette Dickerson, Tazmen Hansen, Marsha Heim, Lori Z. Henry, Debra Liverman, Kitty Lowrance, Dorothy C. McKinney, Thad H. McLaurin, Sharon Murphy, Jennifer Nunn, Mark Rainey, Hope Rodgers, Rebecca Saunders, Barry Slate, Rachael Traylor

Reinforce and assess phonics and word study skills!

www.themailbox.com

ISBN10 #1-56234-913-9 • ISBN13 #978-1-56234-913-4

Printed in the United States
10 9 8 7 6 5 4 3 2 1

Table of

Phonics

Contents

Name________________________________

Double the Bubbles

Write *a* or *i* to complete each word.
If a word can be completed with either *a* or *i*, pop the bubble by drawing an X on it.

1. c ___ t
2. d ___ p
3. h ___ t
4. c ___ p
5. v ___ n
6. p ___ g
7. h ___ m
8. b ___ g
9. p ___ n
10. f ___ n
11. s ___ p
12. s ___ d
13. m ___ n
14. w ___ g

Name ____

Kitchen Duty

Write the short *e* or short *o* word that matches each clue.
Make one change to each word to make a word that matches the next clue.

1. not dry
2. a spider makes it
3. to be married
4. sleep in this
5. ask again and again
6. between your foot and your body
7. a piece of firewood
8. a name for a pig
9. an animal that barks
10. a small, round spot
11. a folding bed
12. corn on the ______

Bonus Box: On the back of this page, write the answer for number 10. Then write at least five words that rhyme with the word.

Name ____________________ Short Vowels

Short *a* and *u*

Scrubbing Buddies

Unscramble the word below each line to complete each sentence.

1. Rosie _________ a sister named Ruthie.
   a h s
2. They have a hard job, _________ they like it.
   t b u
3. They wash dishes, such as _________, _________, and _________.
   g m u s — p u c s — n a p s
4. They start with a large _________ of hot water.
   b t u
5. Then they add lots of _________.
   d s u s
6. With soapy _________, they wash and scrub.
   g r a s
7. Rosie and Ruthie think working together is _________.
   n u f
8. When they're done, Rosie gives Ruthie a _________ on the back.
   t p a
9. Ruthie gives Rosie a _________.
   u g h
10. Their mom and _________ are proud of
    a d d
    their dishwashing daughters.

Bonus Box: On the back of this page, write about something you like to do. Use at least three of the scrambled words from this page.

Name ______________________________

Drying the Dishes

Read each clue.
Write the answer in the ring with the matching number.
The last letter of each word will be the first letter of the next word.
The first one in each ring has been done for you.

1.
t u b
2.
3.
4.
5.
6.
7.
8.
t o p
9.
10.
11.
12.
13.
14.

1. take a bath in this
2. a sack
3. a diamond or ruby
4. more than one man
5. a short sleep
6. "_________! Goes the Weasel"
7. seed in a peach
8. not the bottom
9. a safety __________
10. a pecan or an almond
11. a recess game
12. bubble _________
13. a chart with directions
14. a cat or dog

Name ______________________________

Pregame Practice

To complete each sentence, fill in the blanks to make a word. Use the clue under the blanks to help you.

1. The Wildcats are getting ready for the big game this ___u___ ___ ___ ___.
   (day of the week)

2. Each big ___a___ wants to win!
   (animal with whiskers)

3. First, they practice ___a___ ___ ___ ___ ___ the ball.
   (throwing)

4. Then the team ___u ___ ___ up and down the field.
   (jogs quickly)

5. The ___a___ ___ thing they do is practice tackling.
   (final)

6. Practice is hard work, but it is ___u___.
   (enjoyable)

7. Do you think the Wildcats ___a___ win the game?
   (are able to)

8. You'll ___u___ ___ have to wait and see!
   (only)

Bonus Box: On the back of this page, write three sentences about the team's football practice. Use one of the following words in each sentence: *bat, man, stack, pal, luck, mud, sun,* or *tug.*

Name ____________________

Kickoff!

Complete each word at the bottom with *e* or *o*. Cut out the word boxes and then glue each one in the correct sentence.

1. It's time to get ready to [ ] and cheer!
2. Now we will find out which team is the [ ].
3. Will the Wildcats be able to do the [ ]?
4. The official sets the [ ] for the right time.
5. The [ ] blows his whistle.
6. [ ] the Tigers move down the field and try to score.
7. But the Wildcats [ ] the kick!
8. Both teams are playing really [ ].
9. It's hard to [ ] which team will win.
10. Watch until the end to find out who will finish on [ ].

j __ b	Th __ n	t __ ll	bl __ ck
cl __ ck	w __ ll	b __ st	t __ p
y __ ll	r__ feree		

Name ______________________________ Short Vowels *i*

Having a Ball!

Complete each word to form a word that goes with the matching clue.

1. __i __ __

2.
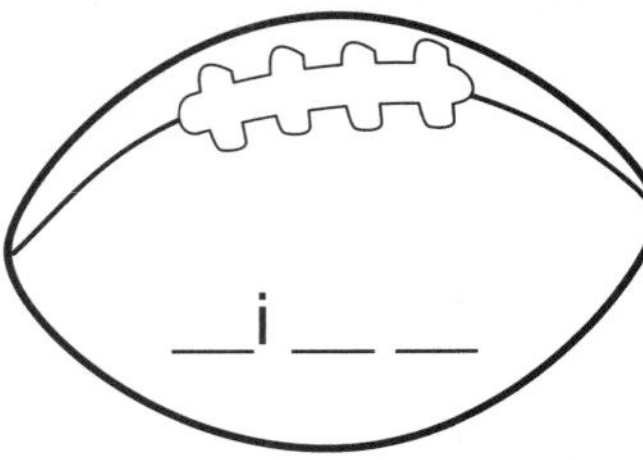
__i __ __

3.
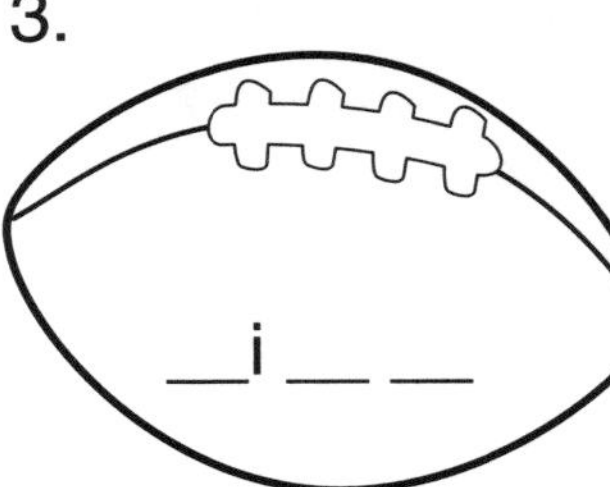
__i __ __

4.
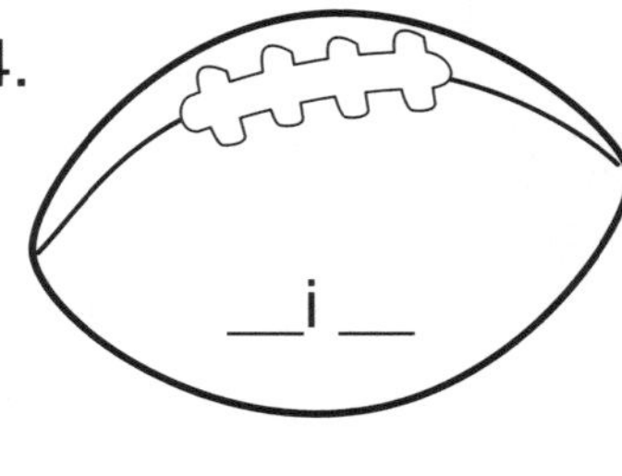
__i __

5.
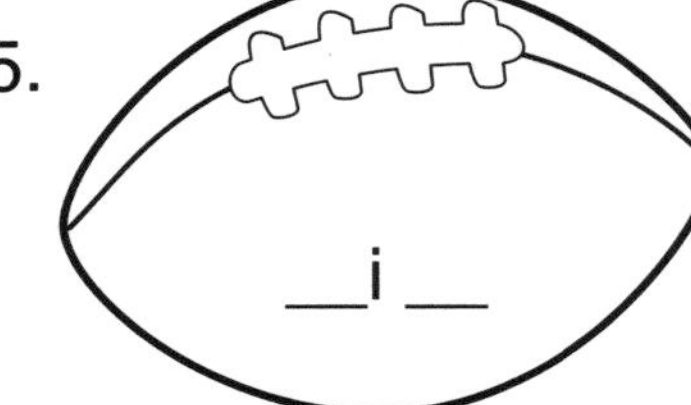
__i __

6. __ __i __

7.
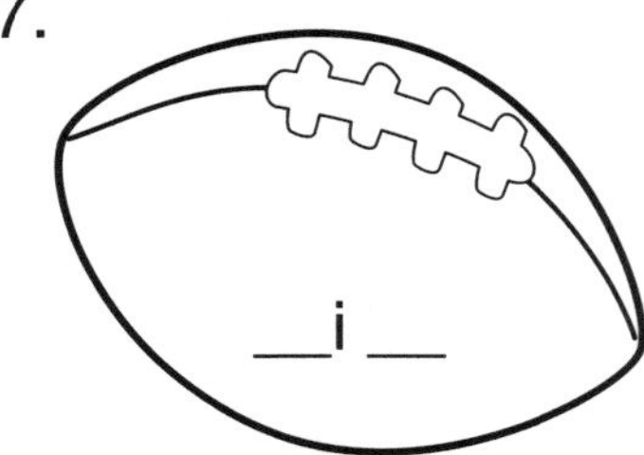
__i __

8.
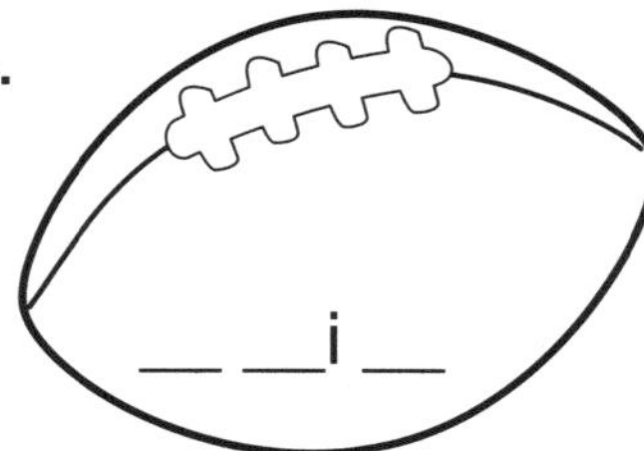
__ __i __

9.
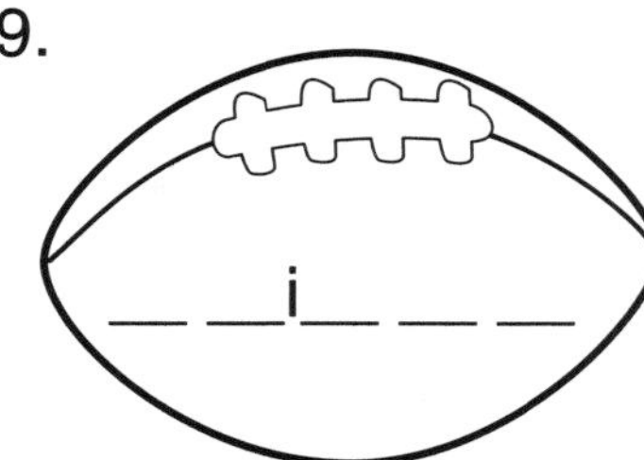
__ __i __ __ __

10.
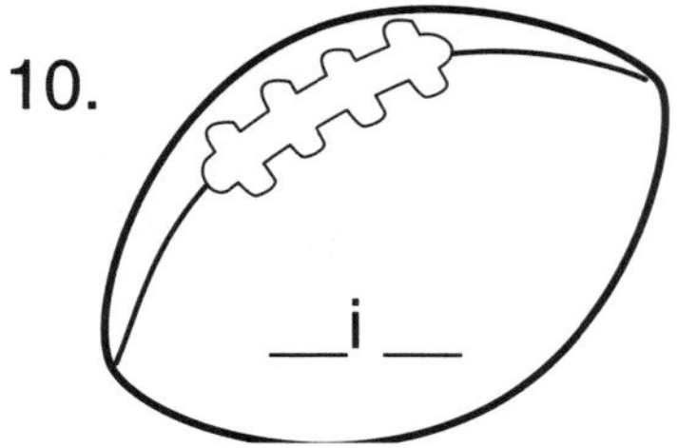
__i __

Clues

1. move with your foot
2. drop or not catch the ball
3. to hope for
4. opposite of lose
5. tear or shred
6. fall or stumble
7. strike with your hand
8. give up
9. trade or change places
10. repair

Name ____

Extra! Extra!

Complete each word on the trophy with a vowel.
(Use each vowel only twice.)
Use the words you made to complete the story.

Wildcats Roar!

It was a close, exciting game, but the Wildcats beat the Tigers by ____________ points. The two teams were ____________ up and down the field all through the game. Each ____________ kicked a field goal. The receivers made many ____________. The quarterbacks threw perfect passes. The players who block were ____________ every play! The crowd stood ____________ and ____________. The ____________ blew their ____________. Everyone thought it was a great game! And even though the Tigers lost, they had ____________ of fun playing!

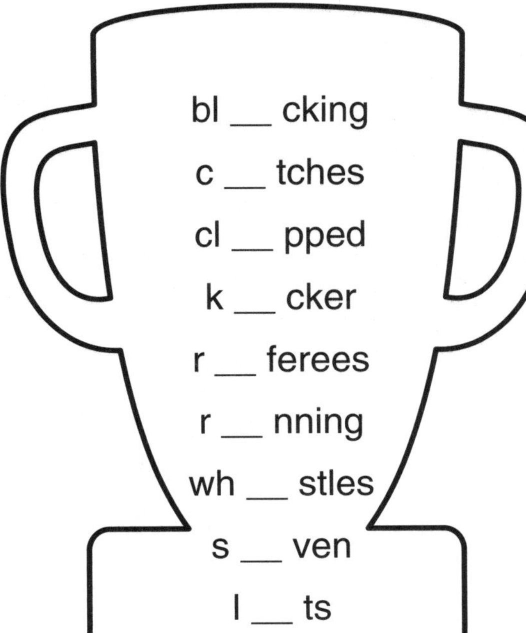
bl __ cking
c __ tches
cl __ pped
k __ cker
r __ ferees
r __ nning
wh __ stles
s __ ven
l __ ts
__ p

Name ____________________

Cookie Clues

Complete the word on each cookie.
Use the clues to help you.

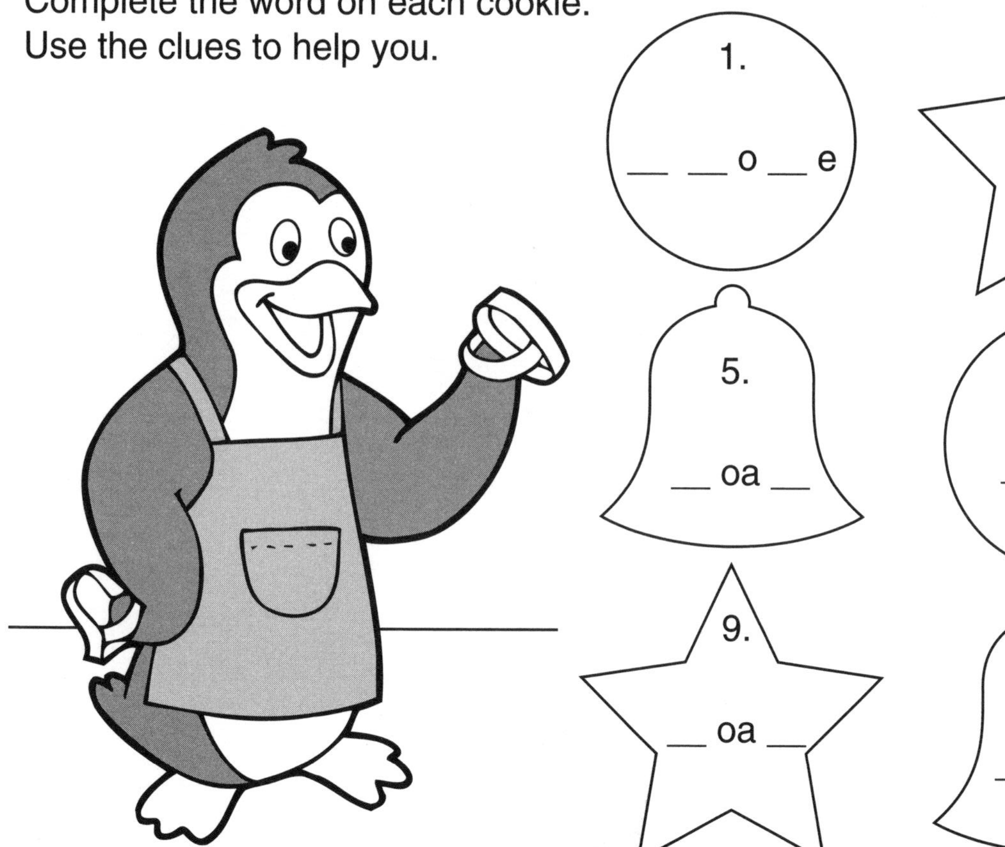

1. __ __ o __ e
2. __ oa __
3. __ oa __
4. __ o __ e
5. __ oa __
6. __ o __ e
7. __ o __ e
8. __ __ o __ e
9. __ oa __
10. __ oa __
11. __ oa __
12. __ __ o __ e

Clues

1. a small rock
2. like a frog
3. what you wash with
4. where you live
5. a street
6. thick cord
7. a treat for a dog
8. opposite of open
9. a heavy jacket
10. a ship
11. a soccer score
12. what you cook on

Name ____________________

Long Vowels
Identifying the long *o* sound

Follow the Recipe

Circle each word that has the long *o* sound.

Cookie Crisps

1. Put butter and eggs into a large bowl.
2. Blend the mixture on low speed.
3. Slowly add flour and sugar.
4. Put the whole mix into the refrigerator.
5. Close the lid.
6. Wait until the mixture is cold.
7. Then roll it out flat.
8. Use cookie cutters to make roses and other shapes.
9. Place the cookies in rows on trays.
10. Go ask an adult to help you with the baking.

Circle one word in each sentence.

Bonus Box: Write three words that rhyme with the word *cold*.

____________ ____________ ____________

Name ____________________

Icy Icing

Color the cookie if the word is spelled correctly.

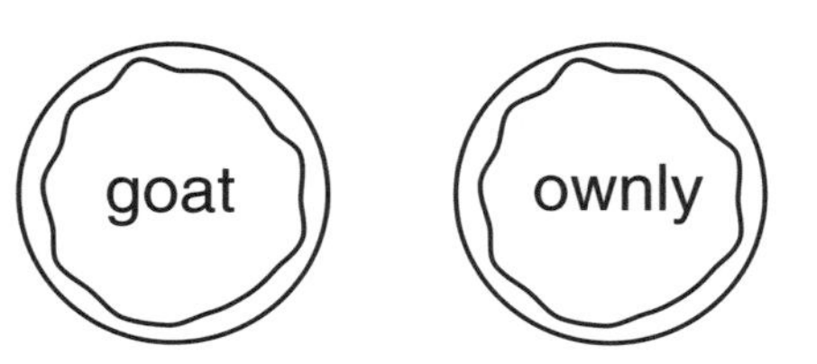
goat
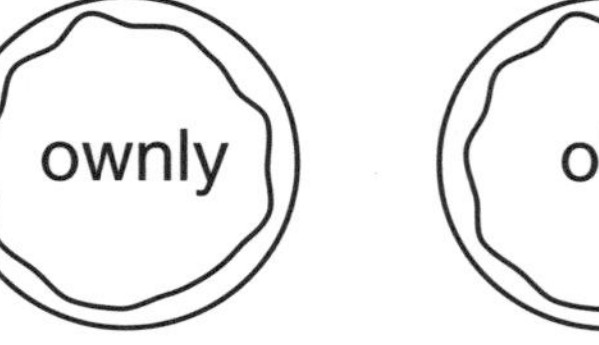
ownly

old

soek
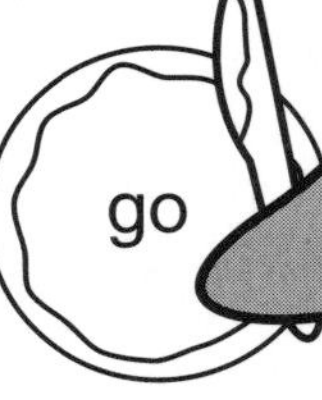
go

hoas

robe

slo

know

loaf

spoke
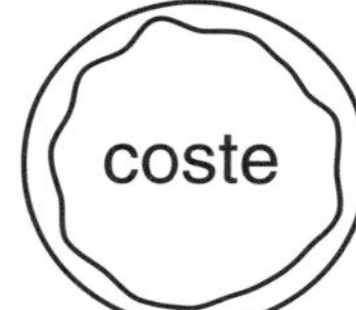
coste

grow

hoap

joke

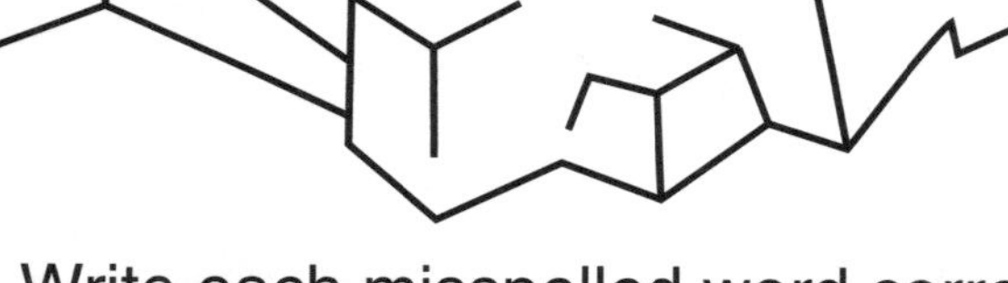

Write each misspelled word correctly on a cookie below.
Cut out the cookies.
Glue each one on top of its misspelled word.

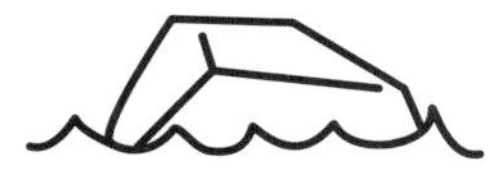

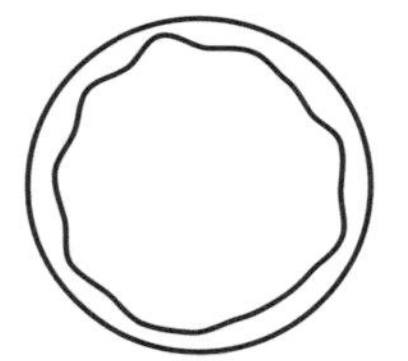
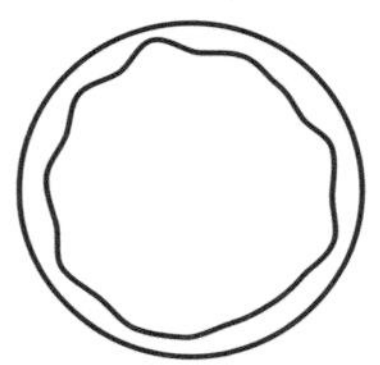
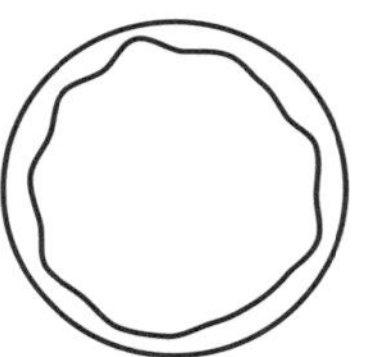
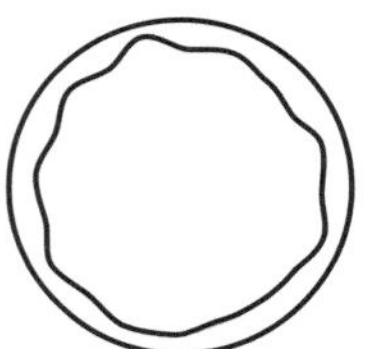
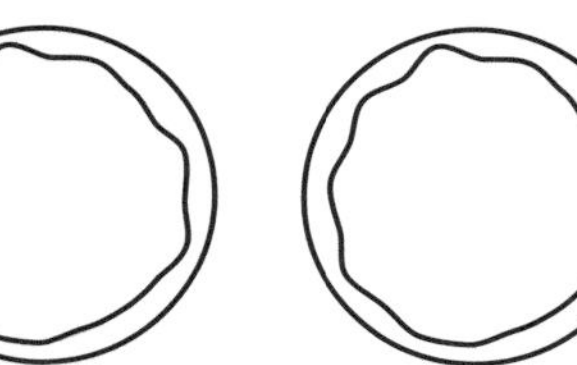
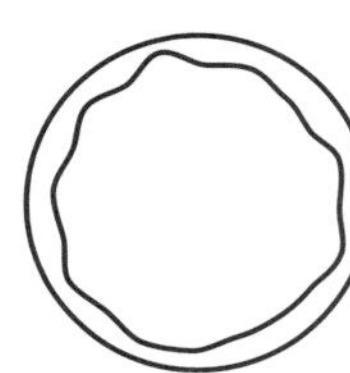

Name ____ Long Vowels *ai, a-e*

Works of Art

Cross out each misspelled word.
Write the word correctly below each crossed-out word.

Crains on the Lak

Paenting the Gait

A Vas in the Raen

Caik on a Plat

A Waeter on Skats

Plains and Treans

Bonus Box: On the back of this page, write three sentences. Use a different word with the long a sound in each sentence.

Name ____________________

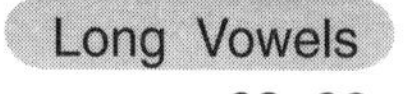
Long Vowels

Fine and Fragile

Write *ea* or *ee* to complete each word.
Circle the word in the puzzle.

wh_ _t	tr_ _	y_ _r
s_ _t	d_ _p	t_ _th
m_ _l	_ _st	n_ _d
b_ _	h_ _p	f_ _l

	o	v	j	m	e	a	l	
q	b	e	e	w	h	l	x	d
k	n	t	m	h	e	y	u	e
g	e	b	j	e	t	r	e	e
y	e	a	r	a	a	h	c	p
h	d	l	e	t	p	e	e	h
e	r	z	f	g	i	a	a	p
	t	e	e	t	h	p	s	
	c	s	e	a	t	f	t	
	b	w	l	o	q	a	e	

Name ______________________________

A Rocky Room

Unscramble each set of letters to form a word with the long *i* sound. Write the word on the line below each set of letters.

grbith
delsi
enim
hgtil
lkei
rpiec
hgint
gihh
snieh
thtgi
diwe
rfihgt
swei
thgis
meic
mgtih

Bonus Box: Circle the words that have the long i sound.
wild kind chip mint

Name ____________________ Long Vowels
Spelling practice

What a Great Place!

Circle each misspelled word.
On the lines below, write each misspelled word correctly.

1. There are many things to sea at the museum.
2. I liek to look at the rocks.
3. Carl likes to see the paentings.
4. Chloe loves to be in the room with the vaises.
5. Eeach of us likes to see the dinosaur models.
6. I like to visit the museum every yeer.
7. Next tiem, I want to see the mummies!
8. I would like to see the cav exhibit too.
9. My brother nedes to go with me.
10. He likes the syte of mummies too!
11. I will ask Mom to taek us.
12. She mite like to visit the museum with us.

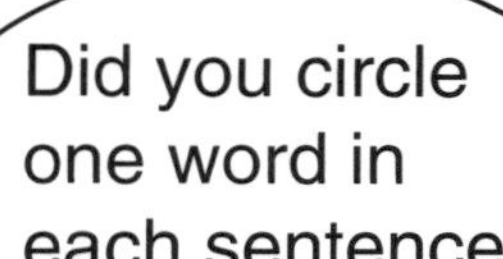
Did you circle
one word in
each sentence?

______________________ ______________________

______________________ ______________________

______________________ ______________________

______________________ ______________________

______________________ ______________________

______________________ ______________________

The Best of Teacher's Helper® *Phonics & Word Study* • ©The Mailbox® Books • TEC61240 • Key p. 119

Name ______________________________ Long Vowels *oa, o-e, ow*

Books to Crow About

Write a long *o* word that matches each clue.

crispy,
warm bread

1. _ _ _ (_) _

what rises
from fire

2. _ _ _ (_) _

to display

3. _ (_) _ _

a warm
jacket

4. (_) _ _ _

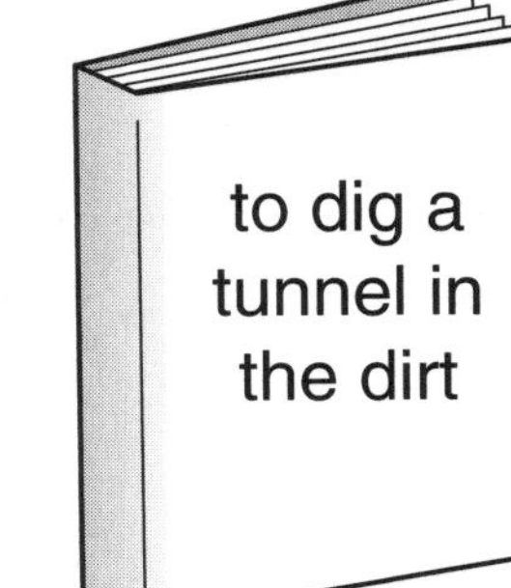
to dig a
tunnel in
the dirt

5. _ (_) _ _ _ _

not fast

6. _ (_) _ _

a froglike
animal

7. (_) _ _ _

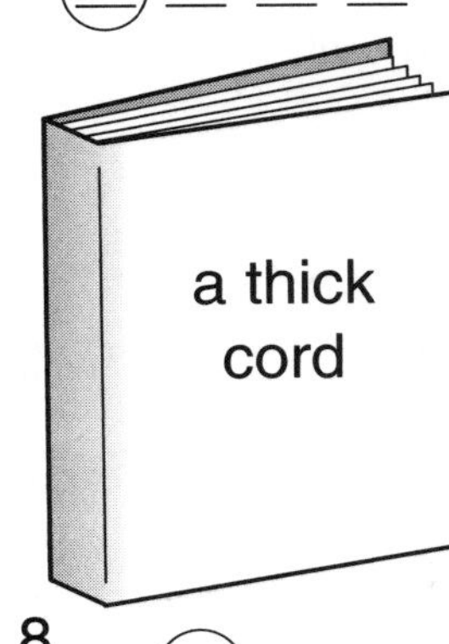
a thick
cord

8. _ (_) _ _

a ship

9. (_) _ _ _

a small
rock

10. _ _ _ _ (_)

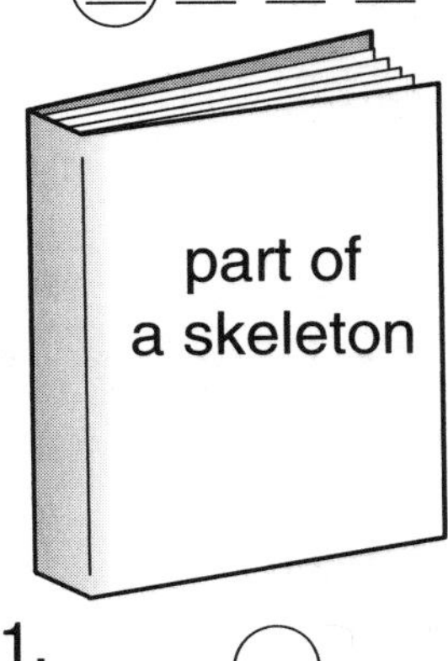
part of
a skeleton

11. _ _ (_) _

a place
to rest
your head

12. _ (_) _ _ _ _

What is Ray Rooster's favorite part of visiting the library?

To solve the riddle, write the circled letters above on the numbered lines below.

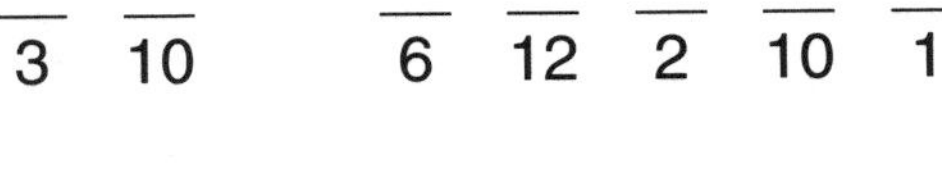

_ _   _ _ _ _ _   "_ _ _ _ _ _ _"
3 10   6 12 2 10 1   4 3 12 4 2 10 11

_ _ _   _ _ _   _ _ _ _ _!
8 5 7   3 12 1   9 8 8 2 1

Name ______________________________

Long Vowels
ea, ee, e-e

Hunt-and-Peck

Underline each word that has the long *e* sound. Some words have been underlined for you.

Ray Rooster loves to read. His class visits the library each week. This time, Ray is looking for a cookbook. He wants to cook a meal using wheat and seeds. Ray looks without making a peep. The book is not easy to find. The librarian, Ms. Sweet, will help him succeed. She knows that they need to check the computer. Together, they'll use it to find what they're seeking. The librarian wheels over a ladder and reaches up to the top shelf. "Thanks!" says Ray. "Our search is complete!"

Find in the puzzle each word that you underlined. Circle the words you find.

j	w	h	e	a	t	b	q	a
w	f	e	s	r	p	e	e	p
h	n	r	e	a	c	h	e	s
e	s	e	e	k	i	n	g	y
e	u	a	d	n	l	p	m	c
l	c	d	s	w	e	e	t	k
s	c	o	m	p	l	e	t	e
h	e	r	e	o	d	a	d	a
w	e	t	a	g	z	c	m	s
h	d	a	l	u	s	h	x	y

Did you find 15 words?

Name ______________________________

Deep Digging

Color the bone if the word is spelled correctly.

todaye
stay
bate
plate
braid
gaim
clay
playe
frame
shaim
raise
fale

Write each misspelled word correctly on a bone below.
Cut out the bones.
Glue each one on top of its misspelled word.

The Best of Teacher's Helper® *Phonics & Word Study* • ©The Mailbox® Books • TEC61240 • Key p. 120

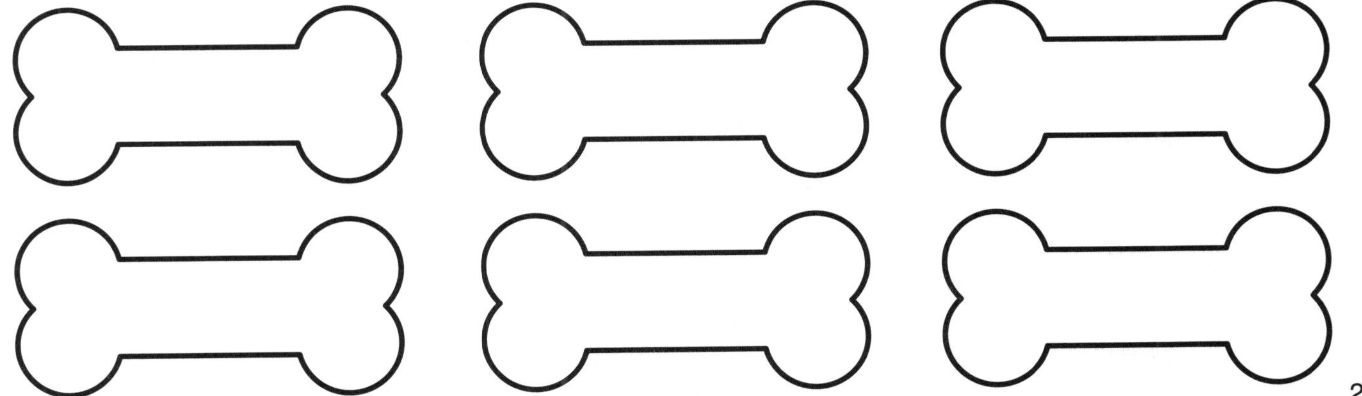

Quite a Find

Read the clues.
Solve the puzzle.
Hint: Each word in the puzzle will have the long *i* sound.

Across

3. correct
5. not narrow
6. let out a low, loud breath
7. a clock shows this
9. not loose
10. the opposite of low
11. part of the leg above the knee

Down

1. a coin worth ten cents
2. after the evening
4. "a ___ old owl"
5. the color of snow
8. strength

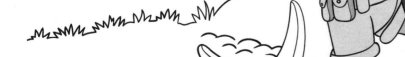

1
2
3
4
5
6
7
8
9
10
11

Name ____________________

Roll on In

Complete each clue with a word that has the long *e* sound.
Use the word bank to help you.
Write the word in the puzzle.

1
2
3
4
5
6
7
8
9
10

Across

2. Gabby ___ about skateboarding every night.
5. He put new ___ on his skateboard.
6. He thinks they will help him ___ higher heights.
9. The wheels will also help him glide ___ cones.
10. Gabby puts on his ___ pads before he rides.

Down

1. Gabby takes a ___ breath.
3. He watches his friends ___ around the skate park.
4. "___ guys are good!" he says.
7. Gabby makes a ___ sweep around the course.
8. He ___ into the air and says, "This is the only way to fly!"

Word Bank

reach	speed
leaps	knee
clean	wheels
deep	dreams
between	These

Name ______________________________

Choosing New Wheels

On each skateboard, write a word that has the long *o* sound. Use the clues to help you.

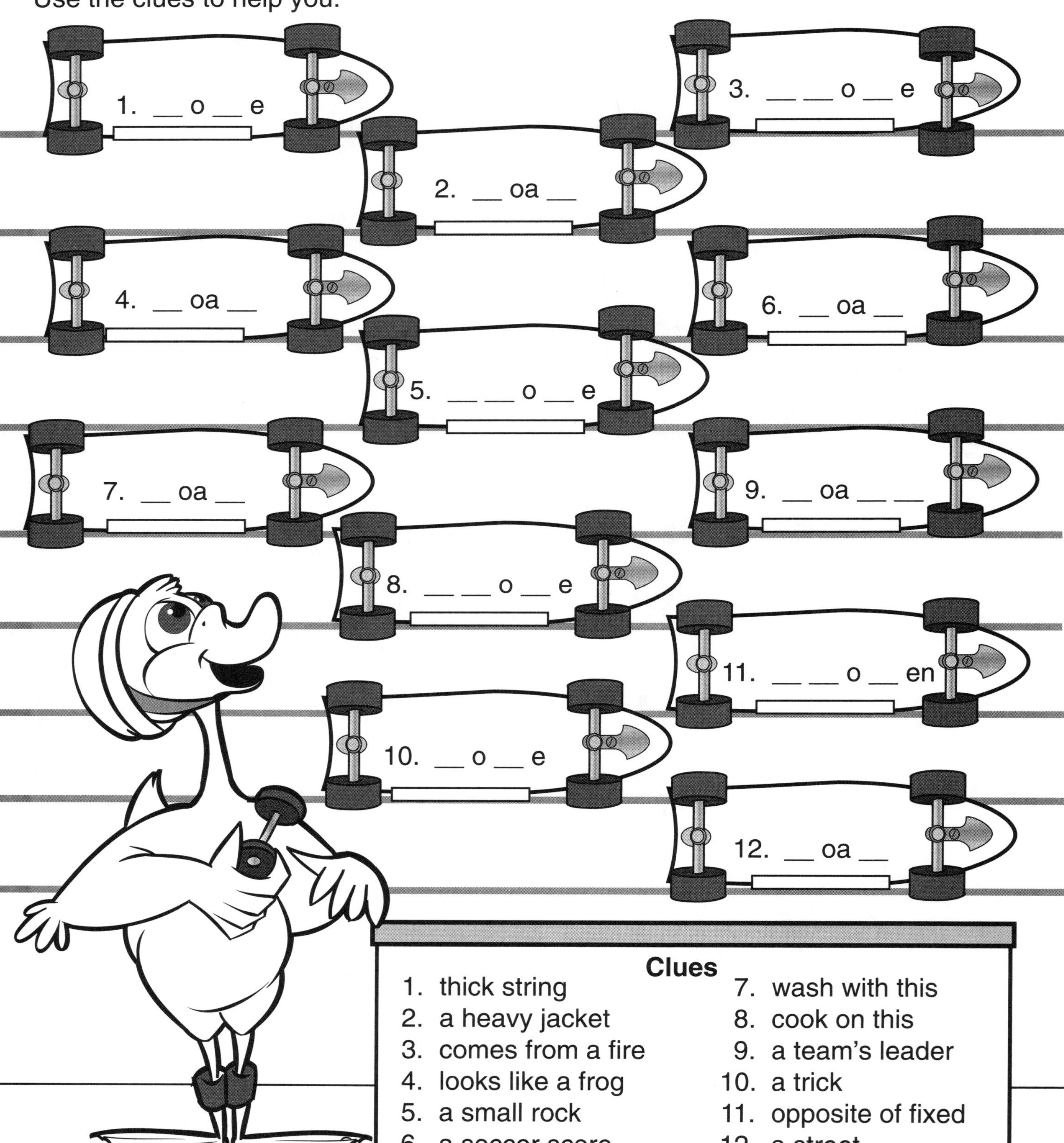
1. __ o __ e
2. __ oa __
3. __ __ o __ e
4. __ oa __
5. __ __ o __ e
6. __ oa __
7. __ oa __
8. __ __ o __ e
9. __ oa __ __
10. __ o __ e
11. __ __ o __ en
12. __ oa __

Clues

1. thick string
2. a heavy jacket
3. comes from a fire
4. looks like a frog
5. a small rock
6. a soccer score
7. wash with this
8. cook on this
9. a team's leader
10. a trick
11. opposite of fixed
12. a street

Name ______________________________

Star Skateboarders

Circle each word that has a long *e* or long *o* sound.
Then write each word in the matching list.

I'm at the home of Gail and Gus Goose. Gail and Gus will teach us their best skateboarding tricks. I am glad they agreed to treat us with a lesson!

Gail will ride first. Her board seems to float in the air as it heads down the street. Watch out for that hole, Gail! The road has a lot of bumps.

Next, Gus will do his best stunt. The nose of his board is pointed straight up. Gus groans as the board flies into the air and then coasts softly to the ground.

Thanks, Gus and Gail! It was nice to meet you and to see those great moves!

Long *e*	**Long *o***
______________	______________
______________	______________
______________	______________
______________	______________
______________	______________
______________	______________
______________	______________
	______________

Board Work

Complete each word by adding ***-ain, -ank,*** or ***-ash.***

1. gr_ _ _
2. th_ _ _ful
3. d_ _ _
4. bl_ _ _
5. fl_ _ _es
6. p_ _ _
7. str_ _ _
8. t_ _ _
9. pr_ _ _
10. str_ _ _ed
11. r_ _ _es
12. r_ _ _drop
13. ch_ _ _
14. c_ _ _
15. b_ _ _ful
16. l_ _ _y
17. eyel_ _ _
18. Fr_ _ _
19. br_ _ _s
20. _ _ _es

Bonus Box: On the back of this sheet, write three sentences. Use a different word from above in each one.

Name____________________

An Acorn for the Teacher

Cut out the acorn caps.
For each acorn, find the cap that can complete all of the words.
Glue the cap onto the acorn.

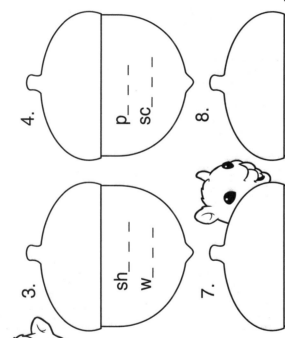

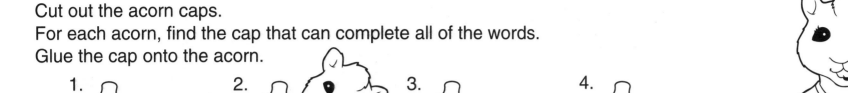

1. h_ _ _ ey
   st_ _ _ing
2. aw_ _ _
   sm_ _ _
3. sh_ _ _
   w_ _ _
4. p_ _ _
   sc_ _ _
5. y_ _ _
   j_ _ _
6. kn_ _ _
   s_ _ _s
7. f_ _ _
   m_ _ _
   sh_ _ _
8. fl_ _ _
   r_ _ _
   cl_ _ _

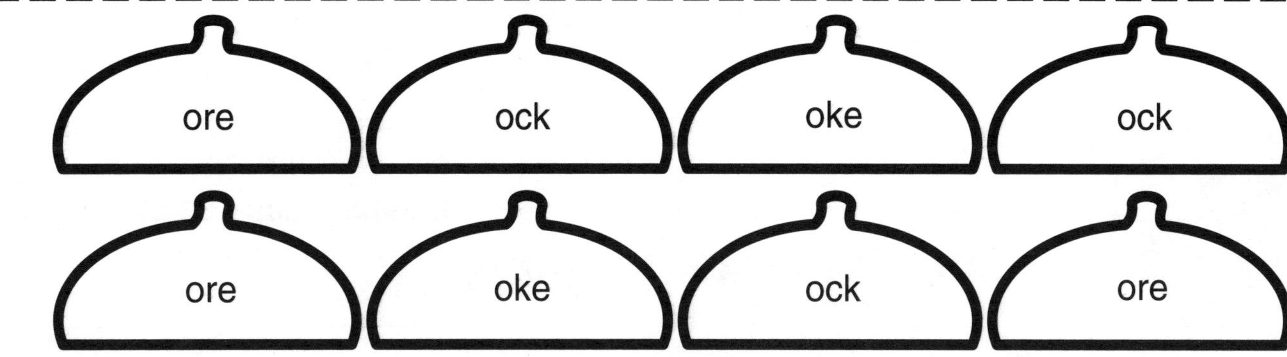

Bonus Box: Complete the sentence by adding *-oke* or *-ore* to each incomplete word.
Mark wants to take m_ _ _ pictures of the seash_ _ _ , but his camera is br_ _ _n.

ore | ock | oke | ock

ore | oke | ock | ore

Name ____________________

A Fine-Feathered Friend

Write the word that completes each sentence.
Complete each word with *-ake, -ame,* or *-ate.*

1. The kids at Swan L__ __ __ School love to eat lunch.
2. They like the lady who m__ __ __ s the food.
3. Her n__ __ __ is Ms. Olivia.
4. Ms. Olivia's lunches have brought her f __ __ __.
5. She doesn't serve the s__ __ __ meal twice.
6. She also loves to make sweet c__ __ __s!
7. Lunch has been busy since Ms. Olivia c__ __ __.
8. Students and teachers line up, holding their pl__ __ __s.
9. Would you like to know what Ms. Olivia will b__ __ __ today?
10. Well, don't be l__ __ __!
11. Hurry to the cafeteria for goodness' s__ __ __!
12. And don't forget to t__ __ __ a tray!

Name ____________________

Stocking the Kitchen

Cut apart the items below.
Glue each one on the correct shelf.

-in

-ip

-it

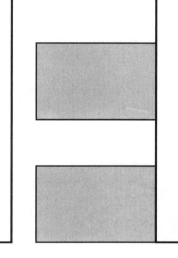

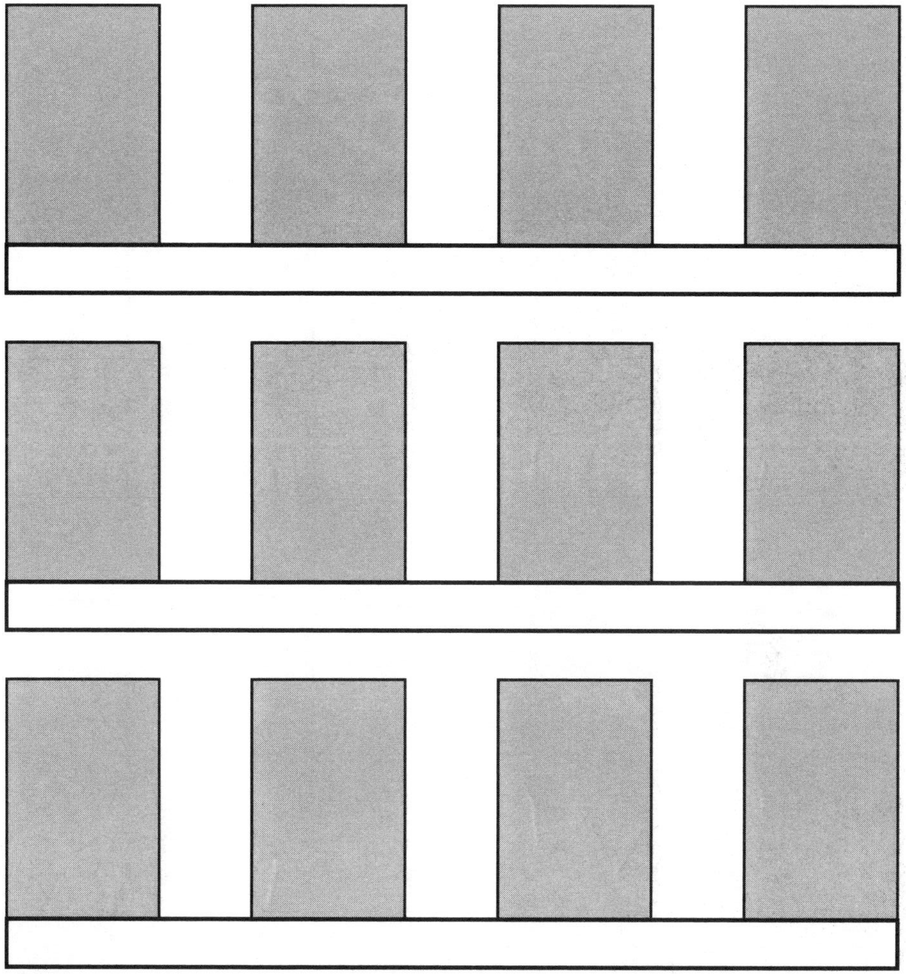

The Best of Teacher's Helper® *Phonics & Word Study* • ©The Mailbox® Books • TEC61240 • Key p. 120

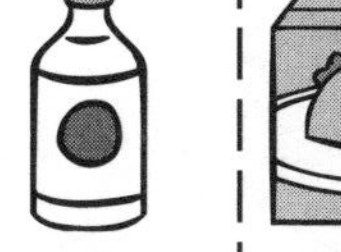

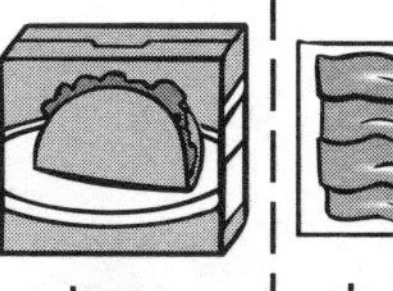
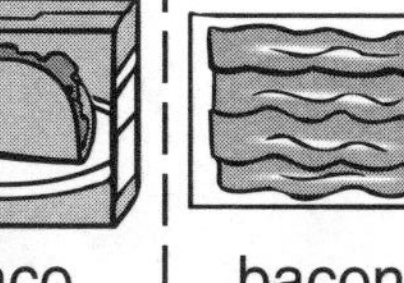
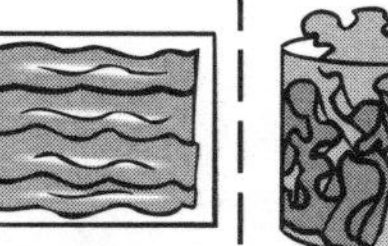

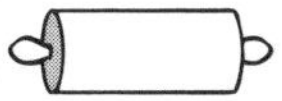

potato ch_ _s	bacon b_ _s	onion d_ _	rolling p_ _	peach p_ _s	pumpk_ _ pie	chip cl_ _s	v_ _egar	taco k_ _	bacon str_ _s	sp_ _ach	spl_ _ peas

Name ________________________________

Word Families
-ide, -ight, -ine

Tricky Trays

On each tray, write a word that contains *-ide, -ight,* or *-ine.*
Use the clues to help you.

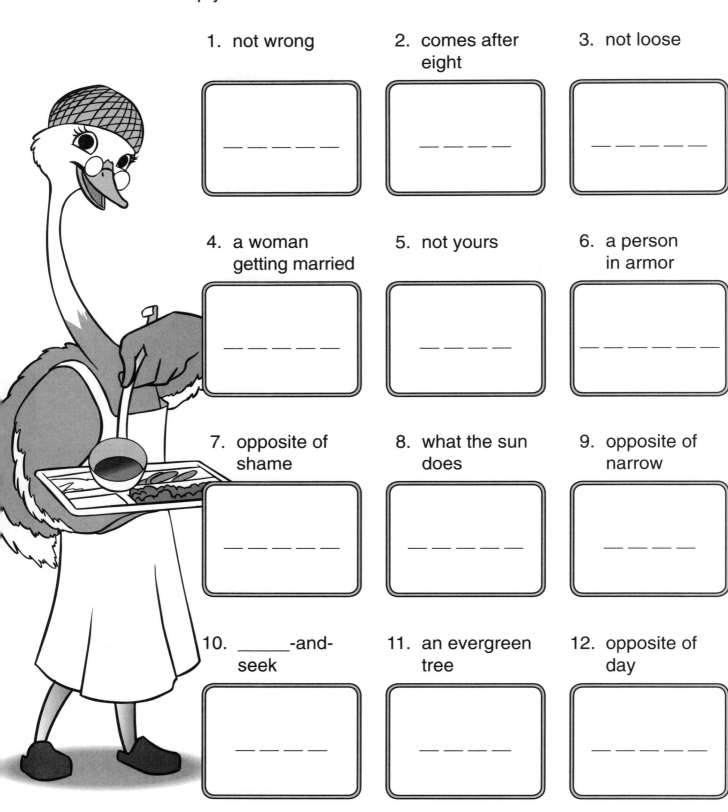

1. not wrong
2. comes after eight
3. not loose

4. a woman getting married
5. not yours
6. a person in armor

7. opposite of shame
8. what the sun does
9. opposite of narrow

10. ______-and-seek
11. an evergreen tree
12. opposite of day

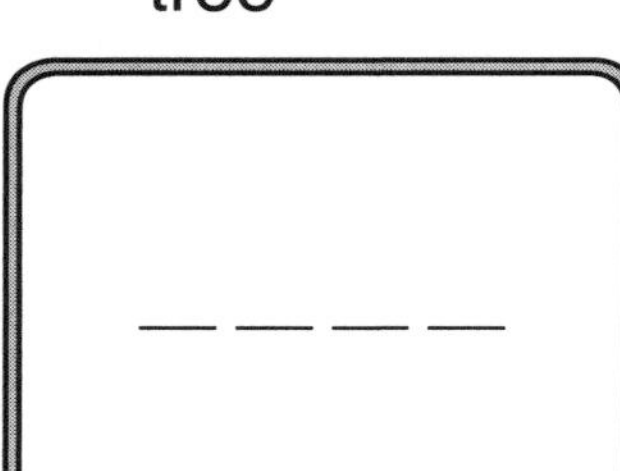

Name ______________________

Soup of the Day

Add the letters on the crackers to the letters on the pot lids to make words. Write each new word on the matching pot. Be careful! Some letters may be used more than once.

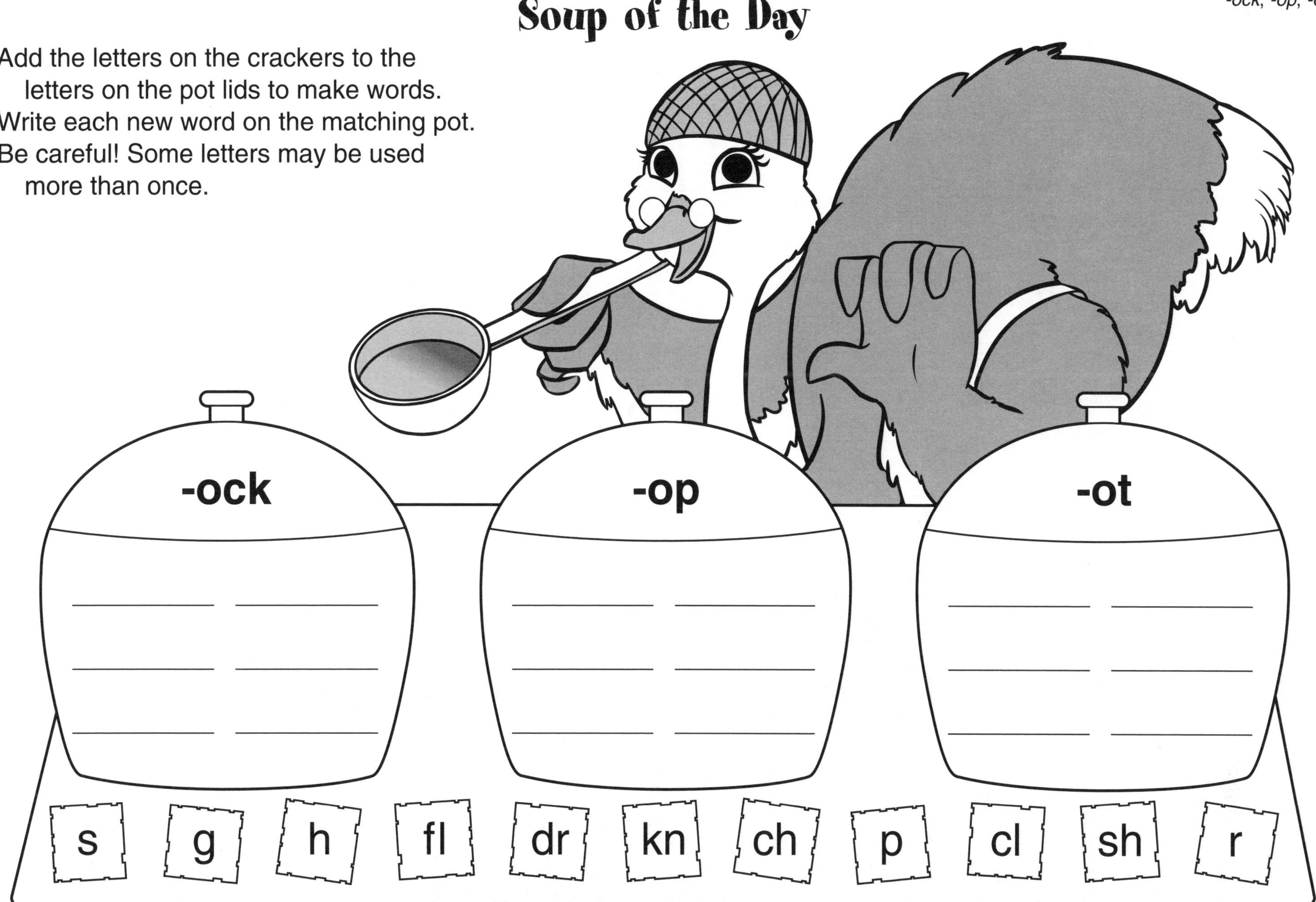
-ock
-op
-ot
s
g
h
fl
dr
kn
ch
p
cl
sh
r

Name ______________________________

Howdy, Partner!

Read the clues.
Solve the puzzle.

-ill Clues

1. the opposite of *drain*: __ __ __ __
2. to make cold: __ __ __ __ __
3. Please sit __ __ __ __ __.
4. a medicine tablet: __ __ __ __
5. *won't* = __ __ __ __ + *not*

-ink Clues

1. what your brain does: __ __ __ __ __
2. the color of a pig: __ __ __ __
3. when one eye closes: __ __ __ __
4. what you do to juice: __ __ __ __ __

-ip Clues

1. a crispy potato: __ __ __ __
2. A leaky faucet will __ __ __ __.
3. turn over: __ __ __ __
4. a large boat: __ __ __ __
5. to quickly clip: __ __ __ __
6. a journey: __ __ __ __

h
p
d
i
r
i
n
h
k
w
f
p

Name____

Flipping Flapjacks

Cut out the butter pats on the left.
Find the consonant or blend that will complete each word family on a pancake.
Put a drop of glue on each • .
Glue the butter pats in place.

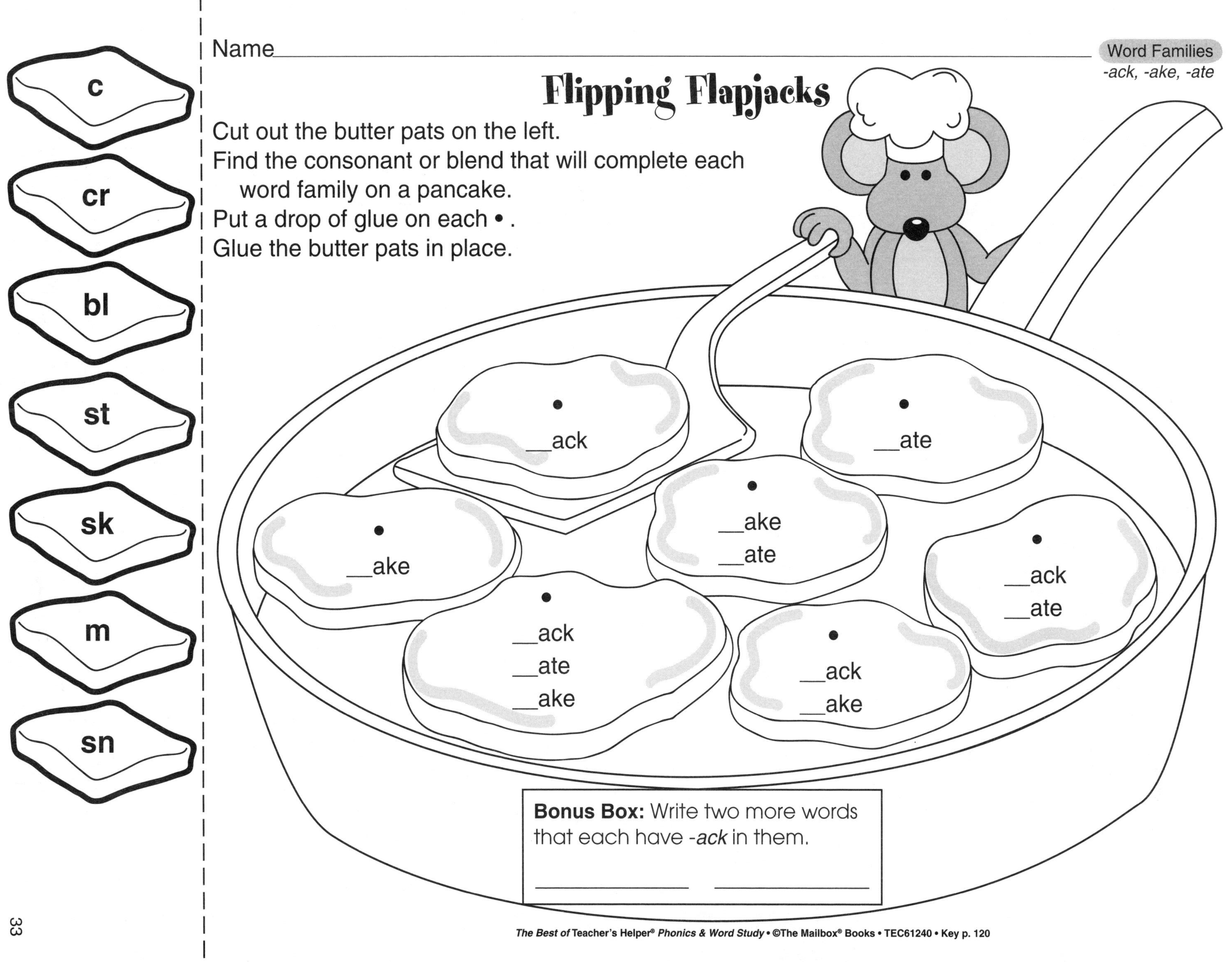
c
cr
bl
st
sk
m
sn
__ack
__ate
__ake
__ake
__ate
__ack
__ate
__ack
__ate
__ake
__ack
__ake

Bonus Box: Write two more words that each have *-ack* in them.

______________ ______________

Name ____________________

Sticky Sweet

Complete the word on each pancake.
Use the clues to help you.

1. take a break
2. dropped to the floor
3. place to sit
4. it rings
5. a snack
6. shout
7. not the worst
8. warmth
9. get money for
10. not east
11. use your nose
12. tidy
13. a bird's home
14. a quiz
15. beef or pork

1. ___est
2. ___ell
3. ___eat
4. ___ell
5. ___eat
6. ___ell
7. ___est
8. ___eat
9. ___ell
10. ___est
11. ___ell
12. ___eat
13. ___est
14. ___est
15. ___eat

Name ____________________

A Spider in Stripes

Complete each word by writing *bl* or *br* on the lines.
Color each stripe by the code.

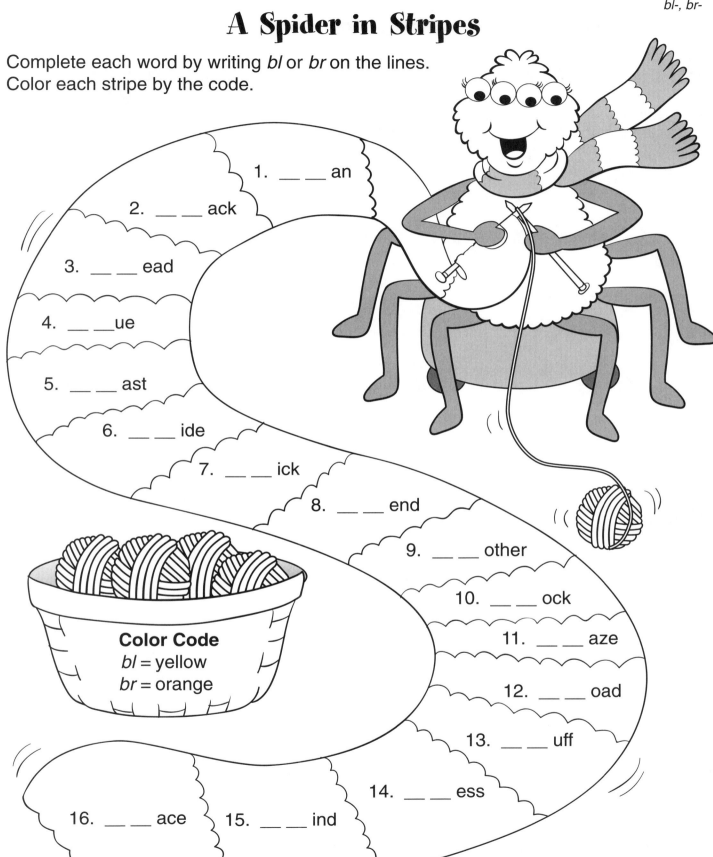

1. __ __ an
2. __ __ ack
3. __ __ ead
4. __ __ue
5. __ __ ast
6. __ __ ide
7. __ __ ick
8. __ __ end
9. __ __ other
10. __ __ ock
11. __ __ aze
12. __ __ oad
13. __ __ uff
14. __ __ ess
15. __ __ ind
16. __ __ ace

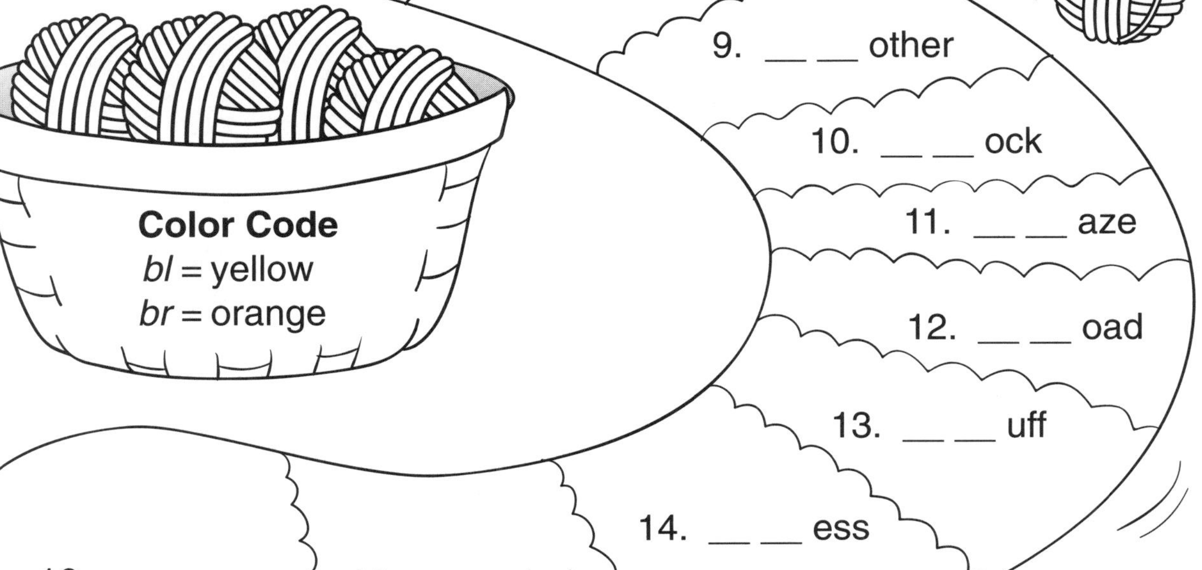

Color Code
bl = yellow
br = orange

Name ______________________

Twisted and Tangled

Unscramble each word and write it on the lines below.
Hint: Every word begins with *cl* or *cr.*

1. b i l m c
2. o r a c y n
3. r m c e a
4. g c n i l
5. o c l s e
6. a c y l
7. c r m b u
8. p i l c
9. f r t c a
10. i c k c r e t
11. c l c k i
12. s s o c r
13. c e n a l

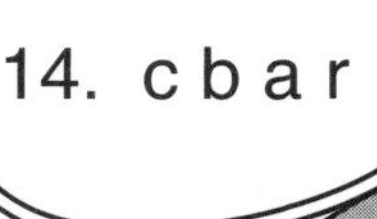

14. c b a r

1.	______	8.	______
2.	______	9.	______
3.	______	10.	______
4.	______	11.	______
5.	______	12.	______
6.	______	13.	______
7.	______	14.	______

Bonus Box: On the back of this page, write one more word that starts with *cl.* Then write one more word that starts with *cr.*

The Best of Teacher's Helper® *Phonics & Word Study* • ©The Mailbox® Books • TEC61240 • Key p. 121

Name ______________________________

Preparing for Winter

Complete each sentence by writing a word that begins with *fl* or *fr.*
Use the word bank to help you.
Circle each word in the puzzle.

1. When the first ____________ comes, Spinner wants to knit.
2. She calls her ____________.
3. The spiders gather ____________ near and far.
4. They sit on the ____________ and get ready.
5. Spinner lifts the ____________ on her yarn basket.
6. Balls of yarn flip and ____________ out.
7. Each spider is ____________ to choose her favorite.
8. Stella chooses a soft, ____________ ball.
9. Sheila gets a bright, ____________ color.
10. Each spider presses her scarf until it is ____________.
11. Spencer ____________ as she knits eight socks.
12. But now she knows that she won't ____________!

Word Bank

frowns	floor
flat	flap
freeze	flashy
friends	from
frost	flop
free	fluffy

a	j	f	d	n	f	g	i	s
m	f	l	o	o	r	f	f	a
f	r	o	m	f	o	r	l	t
e	i	p	b	l	w	o	a	f
f	e	h	o	a	n	s	s	l
r	n	c	k	t	s	t	h	a
e	d	f	l	u	f	f	y	p
e	s	f	r	e	e	z	e	b

Bonus Box: On the back of this page, write a story about Spinner the Spider. Use the words *fluffy, flat,* and *frowns* in your story.

Name ____________________

Sitting and Knitting

Add each blend to an ending to make a new word.
Write the word in the matching box.
Cut apart the balls of yarn below.
Glue a ball of yarn in each box where a word cannot be made.

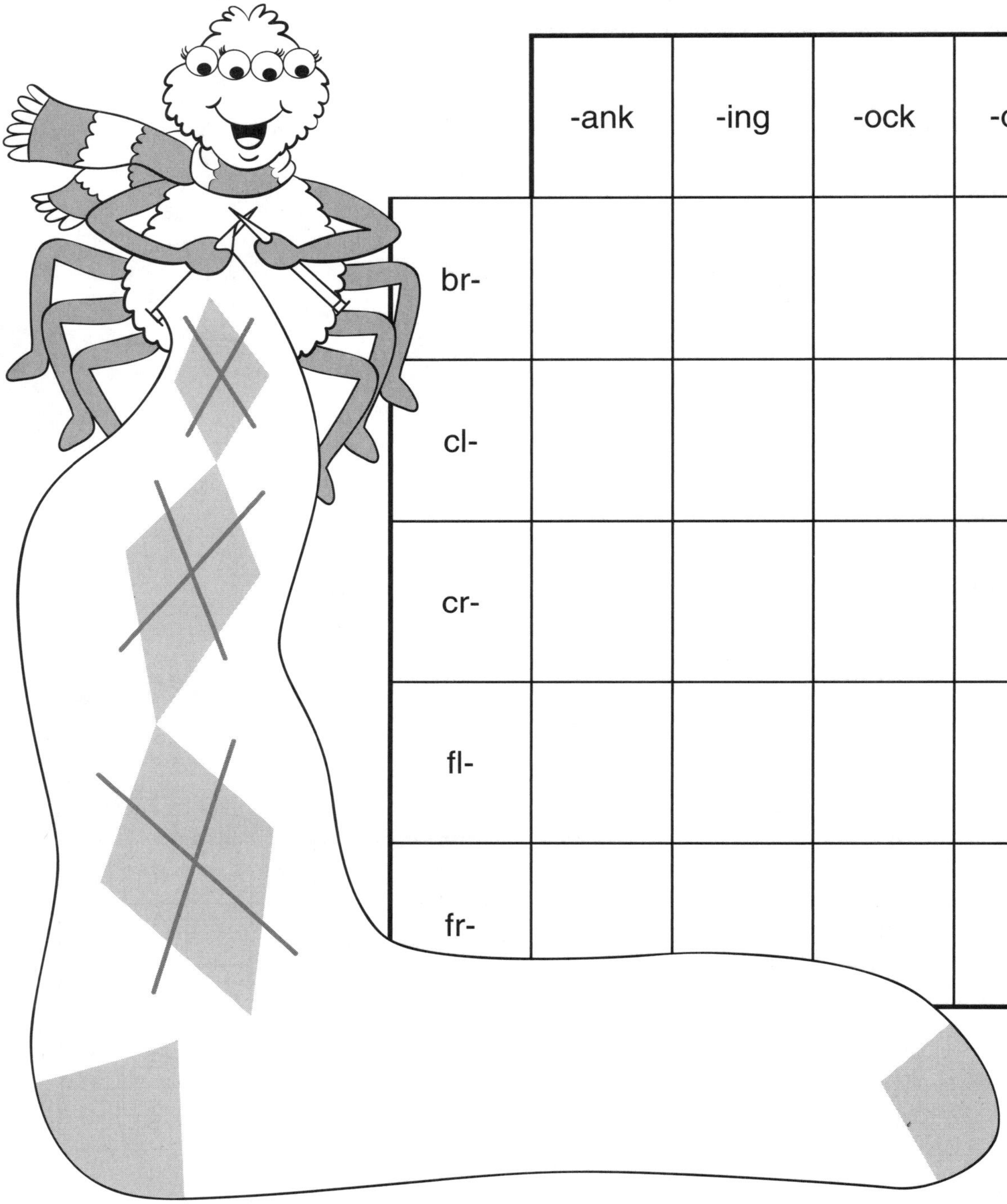

	-ank	-ing	-ock	-own	-ush
br-					
cl-					
cr-					
fl-					
fr-					

Name ____________________

Lessons for Lambs

Complete each word by writing *sc, sp,* or *sw.*
For each pair of letters you write, color a matching book.
One book will not be colored.

___ ___ in
___ ___ im
___ ___ ark
___ ___ arf
___ ___ eet
___ ___ ace
___ ___ ing
___ ___ eed
___ ___ old
___ ___ itch
___ ___ eep
___ ___ eak
___ ___ ary
___ ___ ale
sp
sp
sc
sw
sw
sc
sw
sp
sw
sw
sp
sc
sc
sp
sw

Name ______________________________

Consonant Blends
bl-, fl-, gl-

Read On!

Cut out the boxes below.
Find the shelf with the letters that complete both words on each box.
Glue each box into place.
Write the words on the lines below each shelf.

Library

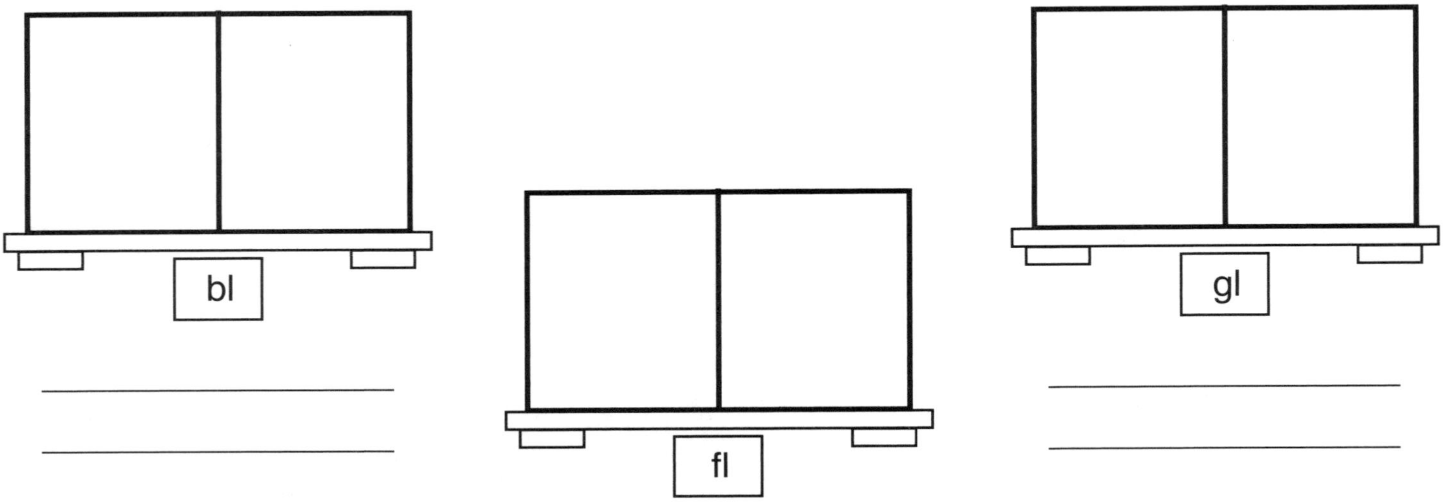

bl

____
____
____
____

fl

____
____
____
____

gl

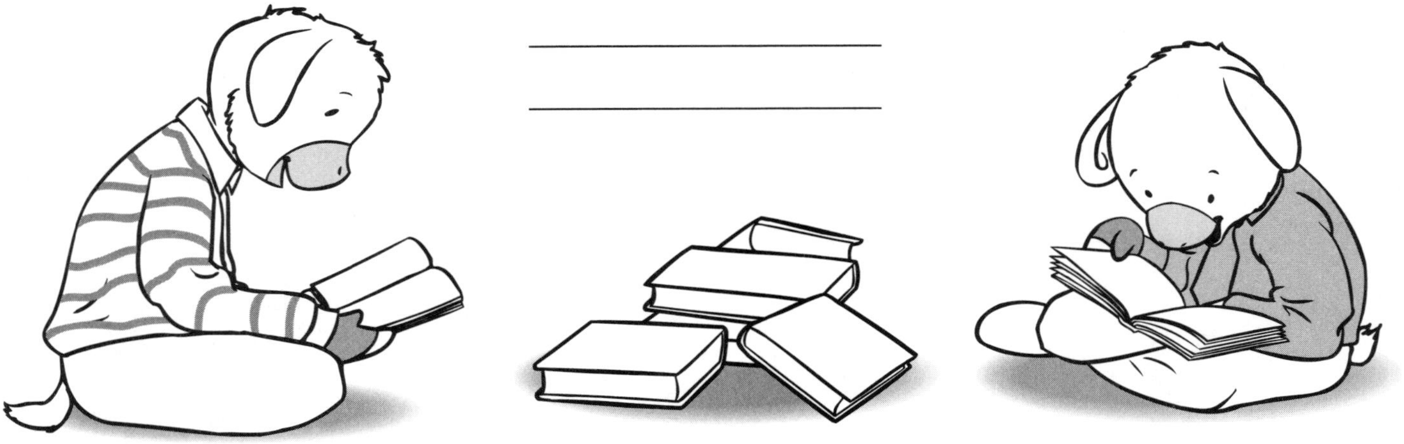

____
____
____
____

____ow	____ap	____ag	____ad	____end	____ue
____ot	____uff	____oss	____ow	____ew	____ee

Name ____

Time for Gym!

Complete each word by writing *br, pr,* or *tr.*
Color by the code.

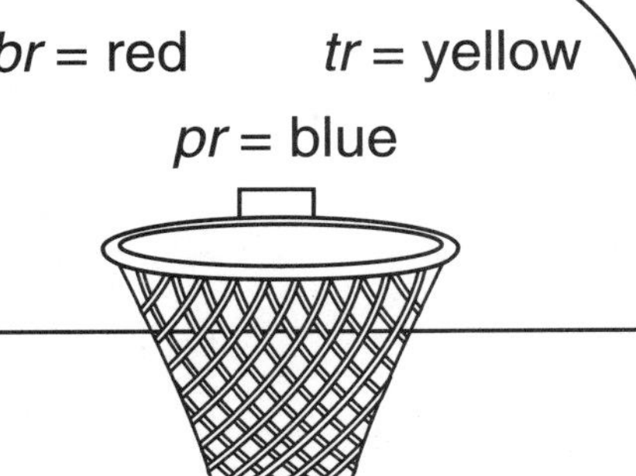
Color Code
br = red
tr = yellow
pr = blue

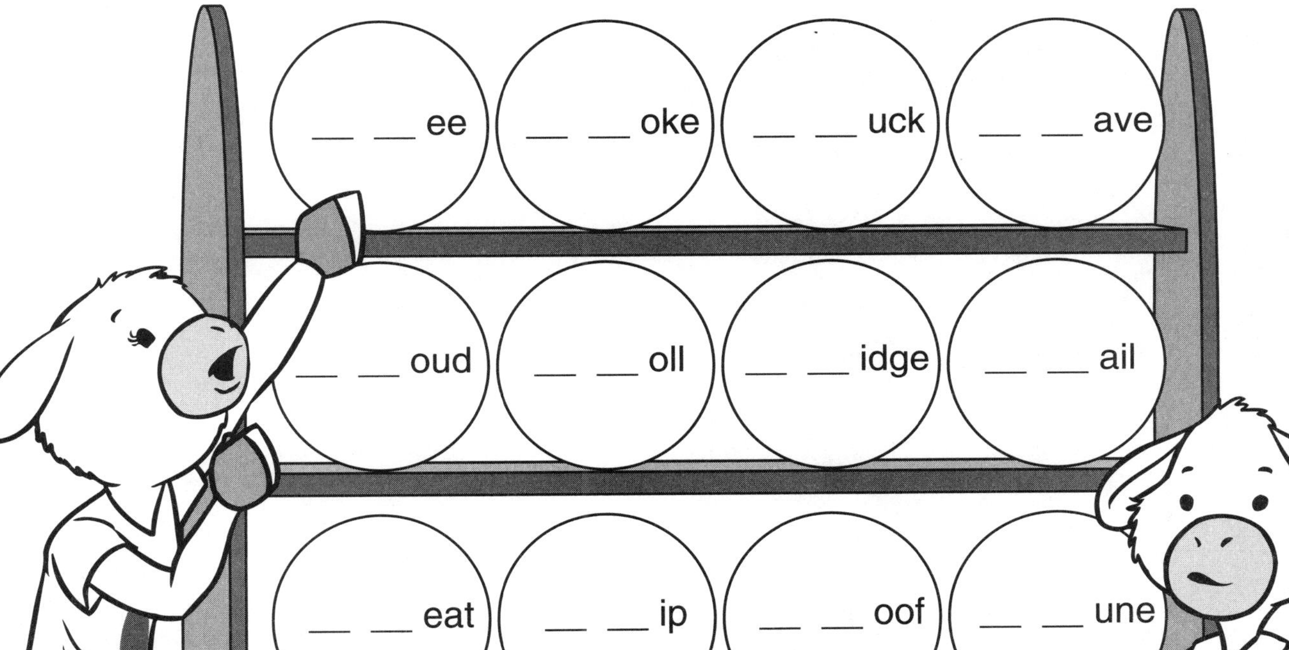
__ __ ee
__ __ oke
__ __ uck
__ __ ave
__ __ oud
__ __ oll
__ __ idge
__ __ ail
__ __ eat
__ __ ip
__ __ oof
__ __ une

Bonus Box: Write three words that each start with *gr.*

______________ ______________ ______________

In the Computer Lab

Complete each word by writing *cl* or *cr.*

1. __ __ear
2. __ __oud
3. __ __ab
4. __ __eek
5. __ __ate
6. __ __oth
7. __ __ean
8. __ __ow
9. __ __isp
10. __ __aft
11. __ __ub
12. __ __y

Bonus Box: Write two more words that each start with cr.

________________ ________________

Name ______________________________

Window Shopping

Complete each word by writing *-st, -ft,* or *-lp.*

HATS FOR HEADS
Our hats are the be__ __,
from ea__ __ to we__ __.
Don't
dri__ __ by,
stop in!
Hurry, hurry while they la__ __!
With these low prices, they're going fa__ __!
Please use
the door on
the le__ __.
He__ __
wanted:
part-time
sales
A hat makes a great
gi__ __!
Beat the heat!
Protect your sca__ __!
All hats are made of the
fine__ __ so__ __ fabrics.

The Best of Teacher's Helper® *Phonics & Word Study* • ©The Mailbox® Books • TEC61240 • Key p. 121

Name ____________________

A Difficult Choice

Unscramble the word on each hat to make a word that ends with *-sp, -pt,* or *-lf.* The first one has been done for you.

pasw
pekt
lgof
pircs
eptcr
pgas
slfeh
lfwo
wetsp
fel
eplst
rpsga

1. wasp
2. ____________
3. ____________
4. ____________
5. ____________
6. ____________
7. ____________
8. ____________
9. ____________
10. ____________
11. ____________
12. ____________

Bonus Box: Color the hats. Use the color code.

Color Code

words that end with *-sp* = brown
words that end with *-pt* = green
words that end with *-lf* = blue

Name ____________________

A Satisfied Customer

Complete the puzzle with words that end with *-st, -pt, -ft, -sp, -lt, -lp,* or *-lf.*
Use the clues to help you.

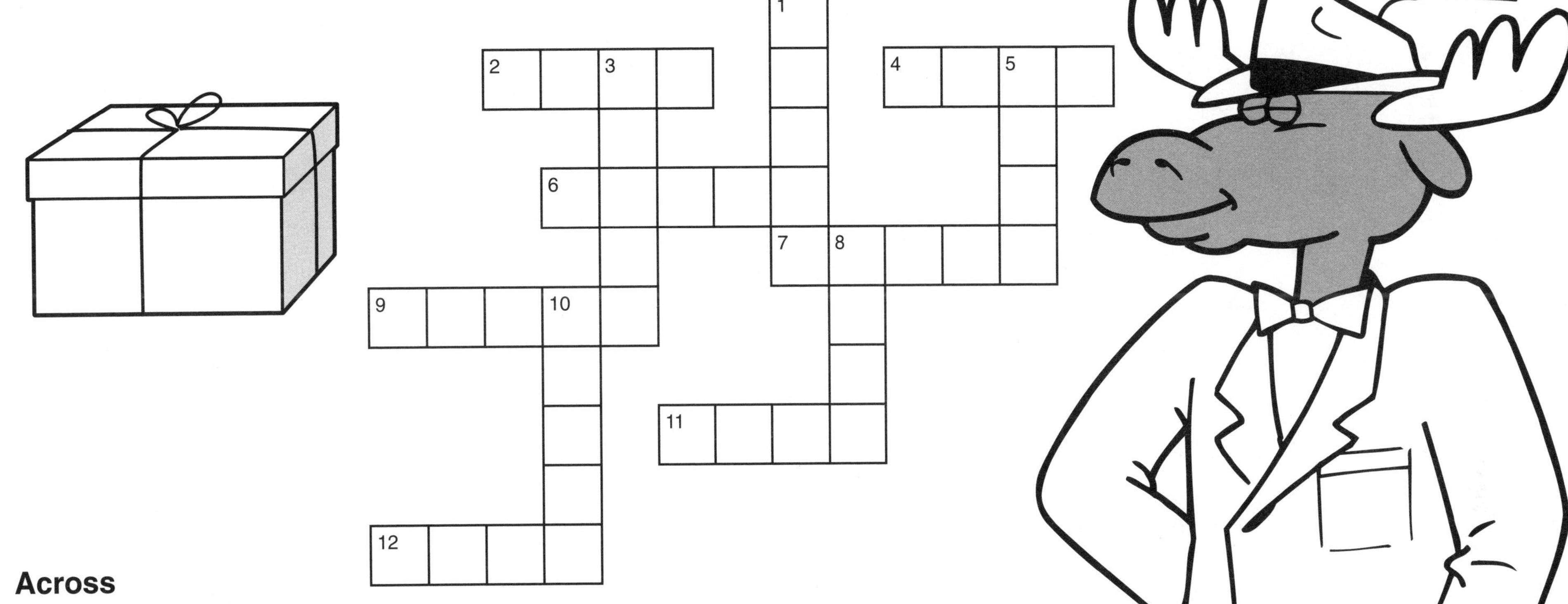
$

Across

2. a small, flat boat
4. the big bad ________
6. crunchy
7. to turn back and forth
9. a thin layer of frozen crystals
11. a hard swallow
12. a sport played with clubs and a small white ball

Down

1. cleaned with a broom
3. before second
5. opposite of right
8. a stinging insect
10. a place to hold books

Name ____

Whip Up a Pair!

Write *wh* or *wr* to complete each word.

___ istle
___ ong
___ itten
___ ile
___ ale
___ ote
___ inkle
___ iggle
___ y
___ eat
___ ench
___ ere
___ ap
___ opper

Bonus Box: *Where* is a question word that starts with *wh.* Write two other question words that start with *wh.* ____________________ ____________________

Name ____________________

Yards of Yarn

Write *kn* or *qu* to complete each word.
Color by the code.

Code
kn = blue
qu = red

___ ee
___ ench
___ ife
___ ake
___ ock
___ ick
___ een
___ ite
___ easy
___ iz
___ uckle
___ ot
qu
kn

Bonus Box: Write two more words that each start with *kn*.

______________ ______________

Name ____

Sorting Socks

Write *wh, wr, qu,* or *kn* to complete each word on the socks below.
Cut out the socks.
Glue each one onto the matching box.

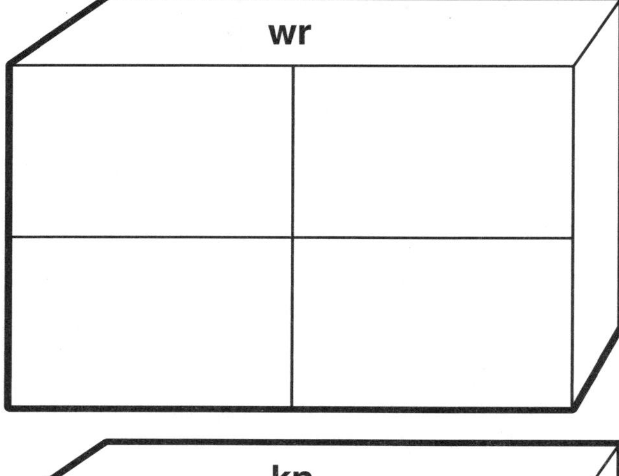
wr

wh

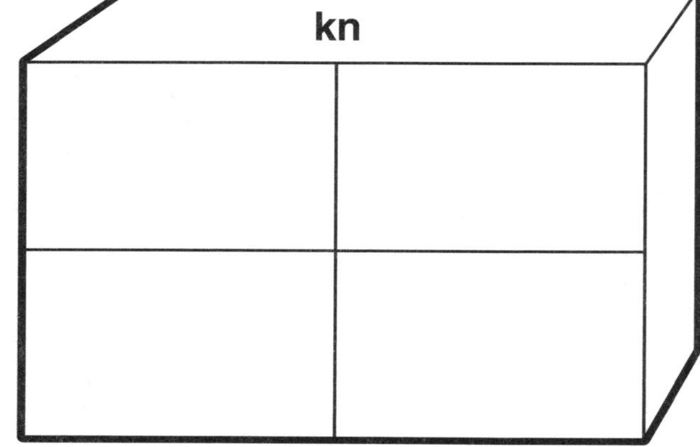
kn

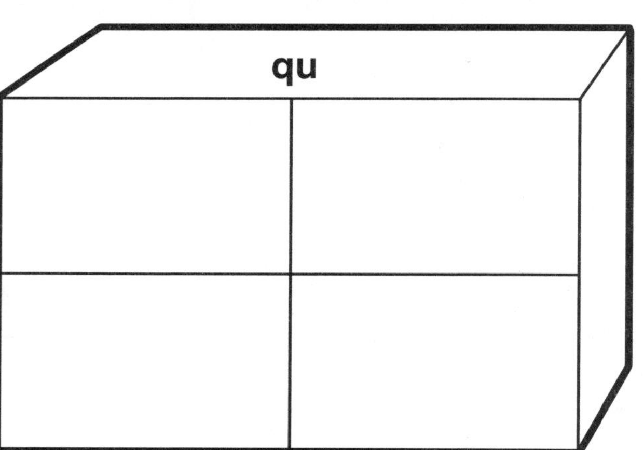
qu

The Best of Teacher's Helper® *Phonics & Word Study* • ©The Mailbox® Books • TEC61240 • Key p. 122

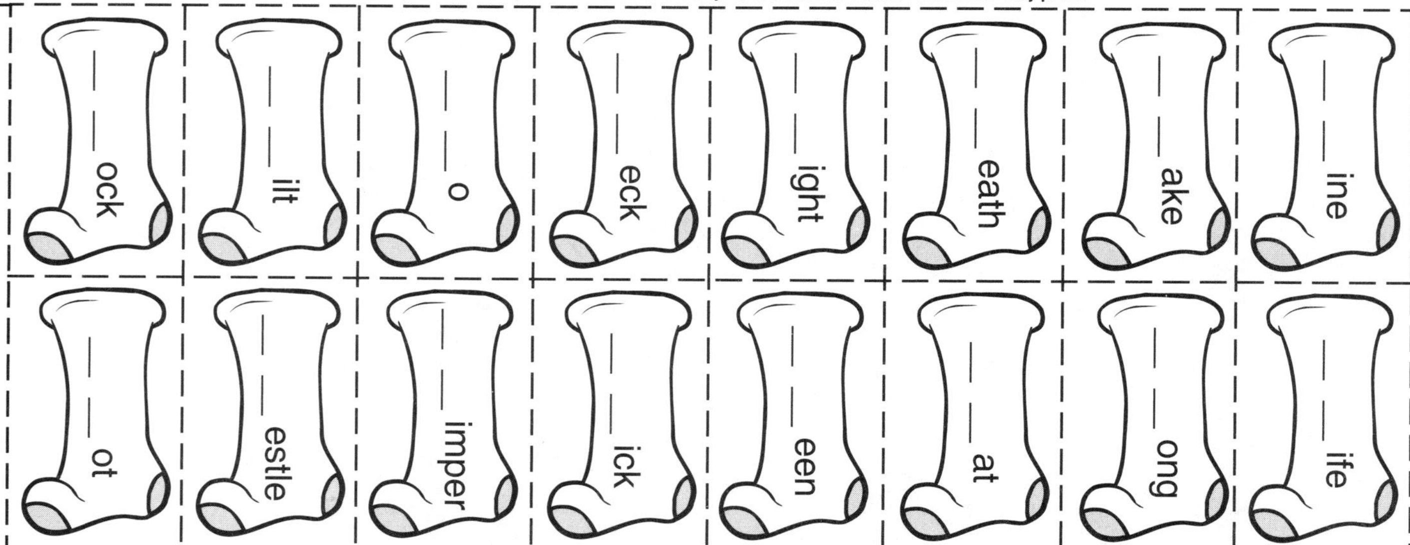
__ __ ock
__ __ ilt
__ __ o
__ __ eck
__ __ ight
__ __ eath
__ __ ake
__ __ ine
__ __ ot
__ __ estle
__ __ imper
__ __ ick
__ __ een
__ __ at
__ __ ong
__ __ ife

Name ____

Flying Feathers!

Complete each word by writing *ch* or *th*.

too ___ ___
ten ___ ___
pea ___ ___
tou ___ ___
mu ___ ___
ben ___ ___
fif ___ ___
wi ___ ___
ma ___ ___
bo ___ ___
bea ___ ___
su ___ ___
pa ___ ___
rea ___ ___
ear ___ ___
lun ___ ___
Cheez

Name ____________________

Look What's Popping!

Complete each word on the bowl by writing *sh* or *th*.
Color a matching piece of popcorn for each ending you write.

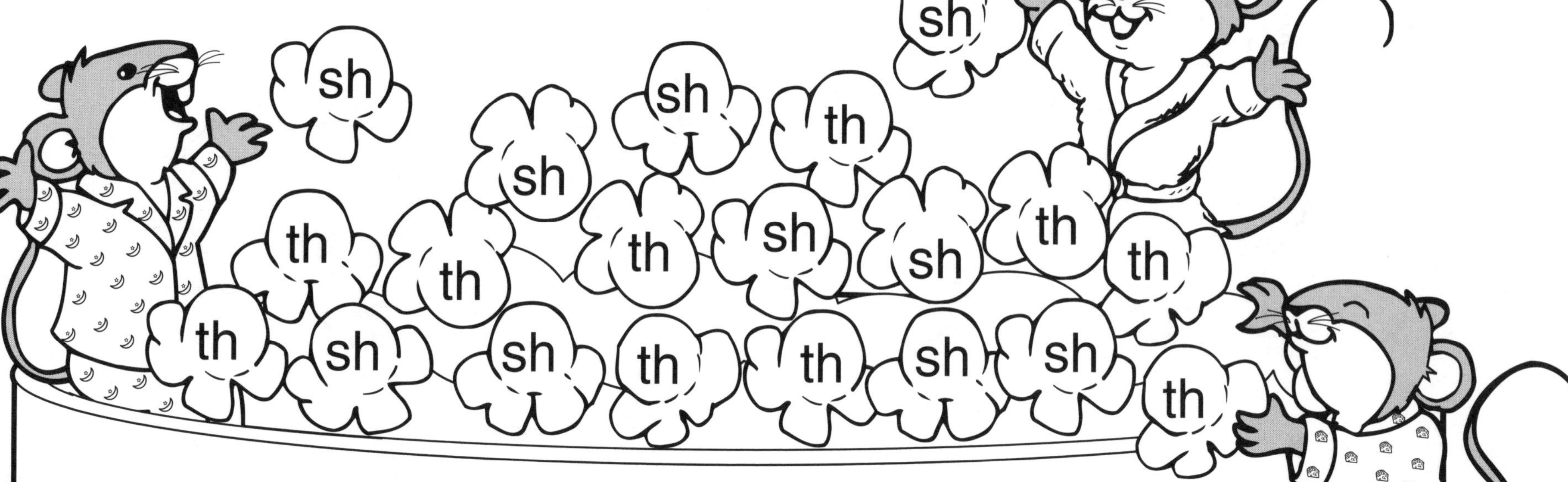
sh
sh
sh
sh
th
th
th
th
sh
sh
th
th
th
sh
sh
th
th
sh
sh
th

1. pa ___ ___	6. heal ___ ___	11. fi ___ ___	16. fre ___ ___
2. fla ___ ___	7. nor ___ ___	12. cra ___ ___	17. mon ___ ___
3. ear ___ ___	8. boo ___ ___	13. tru ___ ___	18. di ___ ___
4. sou ___ ___	9. bo ___ ___	14. bru ___ ___	19. ca ___ ___
5. spla ___ ___	10. clo ___ ___	15. pu ___ ___	20. tra ___ ___

Blast O Cheese
Cheese Flavoring

Name ____________________

Dreaming of Cheese

Read the clues.
Complete the word for each clue.

1. __ __ th
2. __ __ __ ch
3. __ __ sh
4. __ __ __ ch
5. __ __ __ th
6. __ __ __ ch
7. __ __ __ th
8. __ __ sh
9. __ __ __ sh
10. __ __ __ th
11. __ __ sh
12. __ __ sh

1. Rub-a-dub-dub
2. before April
3. has fins
4. noon meal

5. not south
6. sit on this
7. our planet
8. not pull

9. garbage
10. chew with these
11. shrub
12. money

Name ____________________

A Very Hip Hippo

Write **ch, sh, th,** or **wh** to complete each word.
Color by the code.

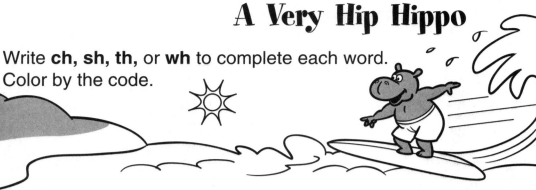

Color Code
wh = blue
ch = red
th = orange
sh = green

__ __ ales

__ __ irty

__ __ ecks

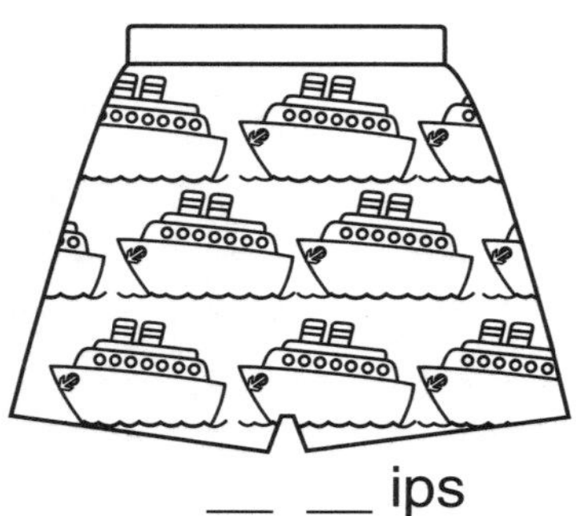

__ __ ips

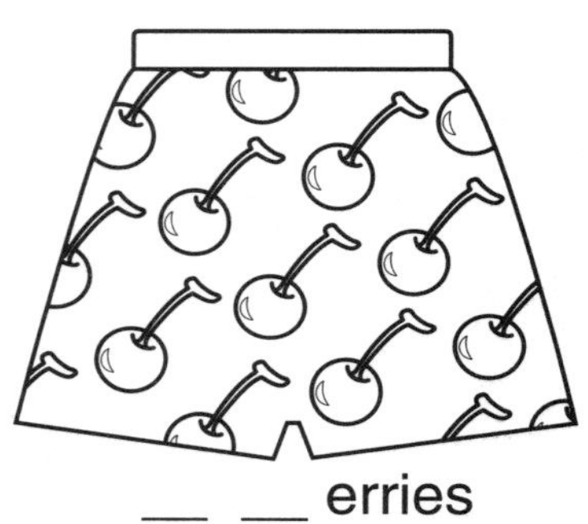

__ __ erries

__ __ eels

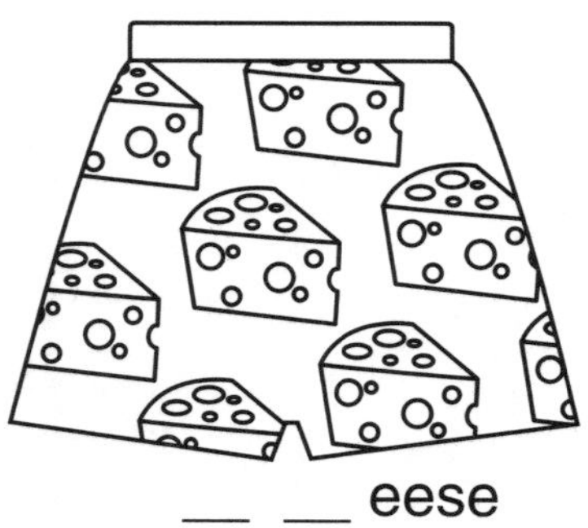

__ __ eese

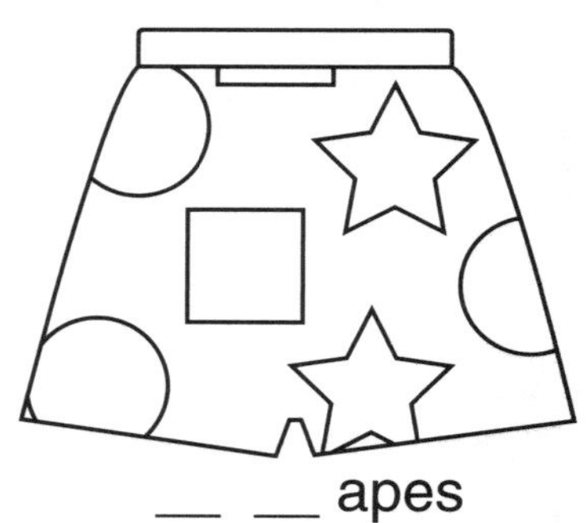

__ __ apes

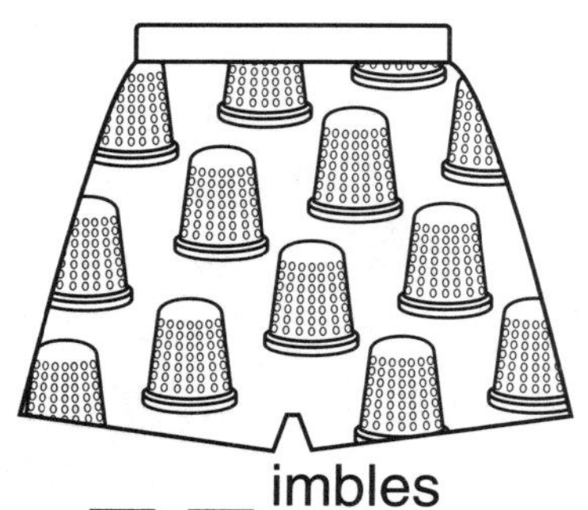

__ __ imbles

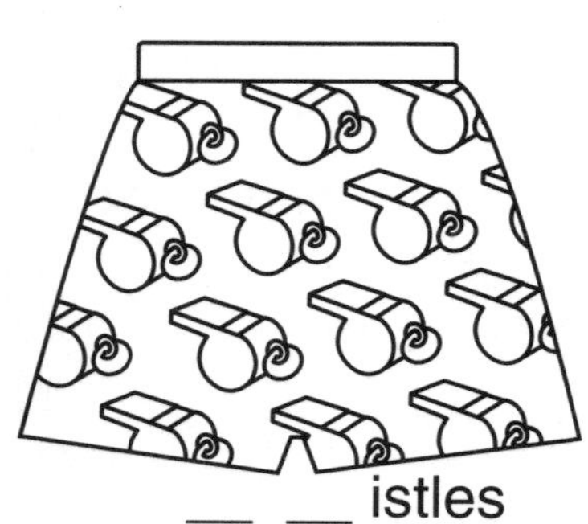

__ __ istles

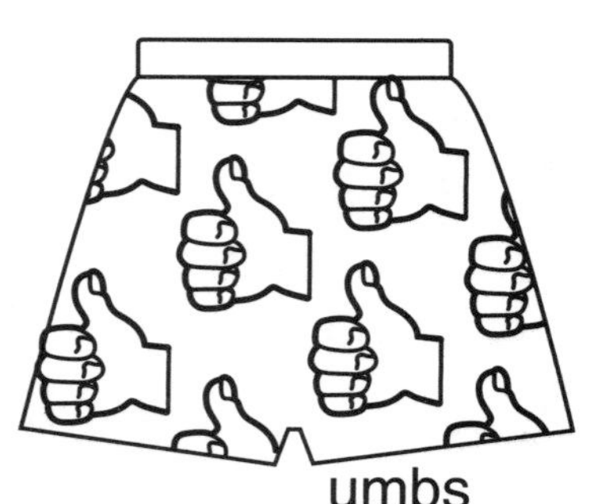

__ __ umbs

__ __ eep

The Best of Teacher's Helper® *Phonics & Word Study* • ©The Mailbox® Books • TEC61240 • Key p. 122

Name ______________________________

Surfing in Style

Write **ch, sh,** or **th** to complete each word.

1. Once a mon __ __, Hugo goes surfing.
2. He always goes wi __ __ his best friend, Harry.
3. They like surfing because it's good for their heal __ __.
4. But they love surfing because it's su __ __ fun!
5. When they get to the bea __ __, they grab their surfboards.
6. Then they bo __ __ race to the waves.
7. People stare as they ru __ __ toward the water.
8. Then, with a spla __ __, they're in!
9. Even the fi __ __ stop to watch Hugo and Harry.
10. But it's not their surfing that everyone enjoys so mu __ __.
11. Can you guess the tru __ __?
12. It's their wild and styli __ __ swimming trunks!

Name ____________________

Colorful Surfboard

On the towel, write the word for each picture.
Circle the consonant digraph in each word.
Then write each word on the correct part of the sand castle.

1. ________
2. ________
3. ________
4. ________
5. ________
6. ________
7. ________
8. ________
9. ________
10. ________

Surfboard pictures: 1. 2. 3. 4. 5. 6. 13 7. 8. 9. 10.

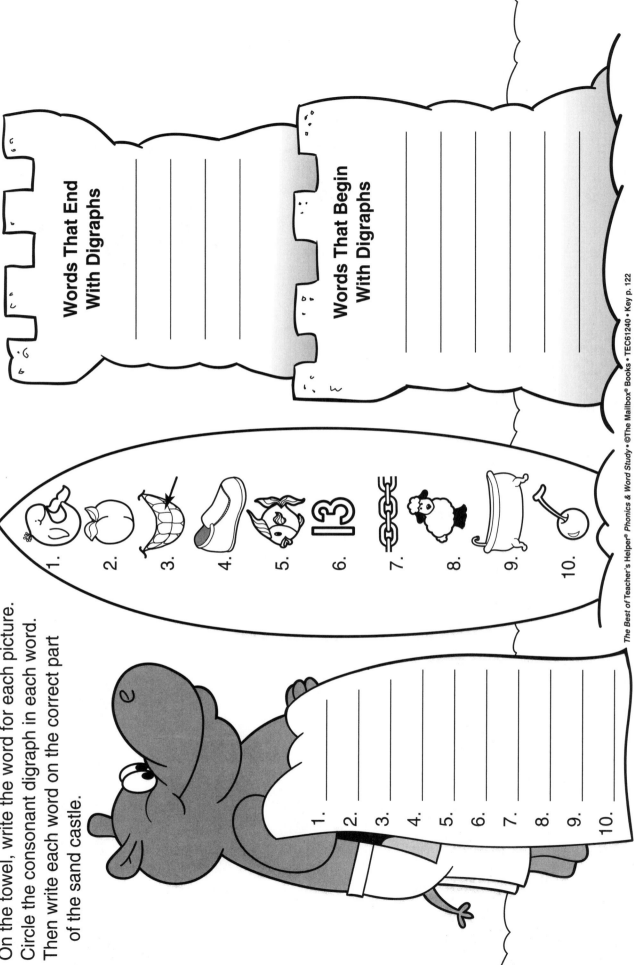

Words That End With Digraphs

____
____
____
____

Words That Begin With Digraphs

____
____
____
____
____
____

Name________________________________

Make a Splash!

Write *ai* or *ay* to complete each word.
Color by the code.

Color Code
ai = blue
ay = yellow

How do my friends and I feel about swimming in the pool?

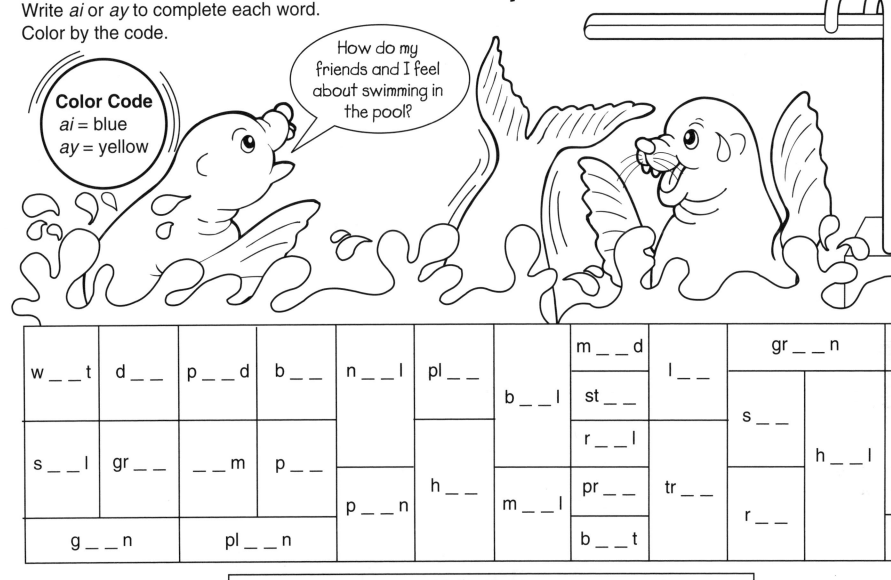

w _ _ t
s _ _ l
d _ _
gr _ _
g _ _ n
p _ _ d
_ _ m
b _ _
p _ _
pl _ _ n
n _ _ l
p _ _ n
pl _ _
h _ _
b _ _ l
m _ _ l
m _ _ d
st _ _
r _ _ l
pr _ _
b _ _ t
l _ _
tr _ _
gr _ _ n
s _ _
r _ _
h _ _ l
r _ _ n
w _ _
m _ _

Bonus Box: Write two more words that each have *ay*.

______________________ ______________________

Name ____

Pool Party

For each clue, write a word that has *oa* or *ue.*

1. the color of a cloudless sky
2. a small ship
3. a street
4. the opposite of false
5. a ball __________ on the water
6. a hint
7. a farm animal with horns
8. gasoline
9. a warm and crispy bread slice
10. sticky white liquid
11. used in the bathtub
12. a jacket

1. b ___ ___ ___
2. b ___ ___ ___
3. r ___ ___ ___
4. t ___ ___ ___
5. f ___ ___ ___ ___ ___
6. c ___ ___ ___
7. g ___ ___ ___
8. f ___ ___ ___
9. t ___ ___ ___ ___
10. g ___ ___ ___
11. s ___ ___ ___
12. c ___ ___ ___

Bonus Box: On the back of this page, write a paragraph about the seals' pool party. Use at least three of the words on the pool in your paragraph.

Name______________________

Have a Ball!

Write *ai, ay, oa,* or *ue* to complete each word.
Color by the code.

Color Code
ai = green
ay = yellow
oa = red
ue = blue

s _ _ p
m _ _ d
bl _ _
m _ _ or
tod _ _
fl _ _ t
c _ _ t
gl _ _
b _ _
p _ _ nt
d _ _ sy
tr _ _ s
s _ _ l
p _ _
spr _ _
r _ _ d
untr _ _
n _ _ l
cr _ _ l
m _ _ be
gr _ _
t _ _ st
pl _ _ n
repl _ _

Name ____________________

Hot on the Trail

Complete each word by writing *ai* or *ay.*
Cut apart the word cards.
Glue each card on a matching square.

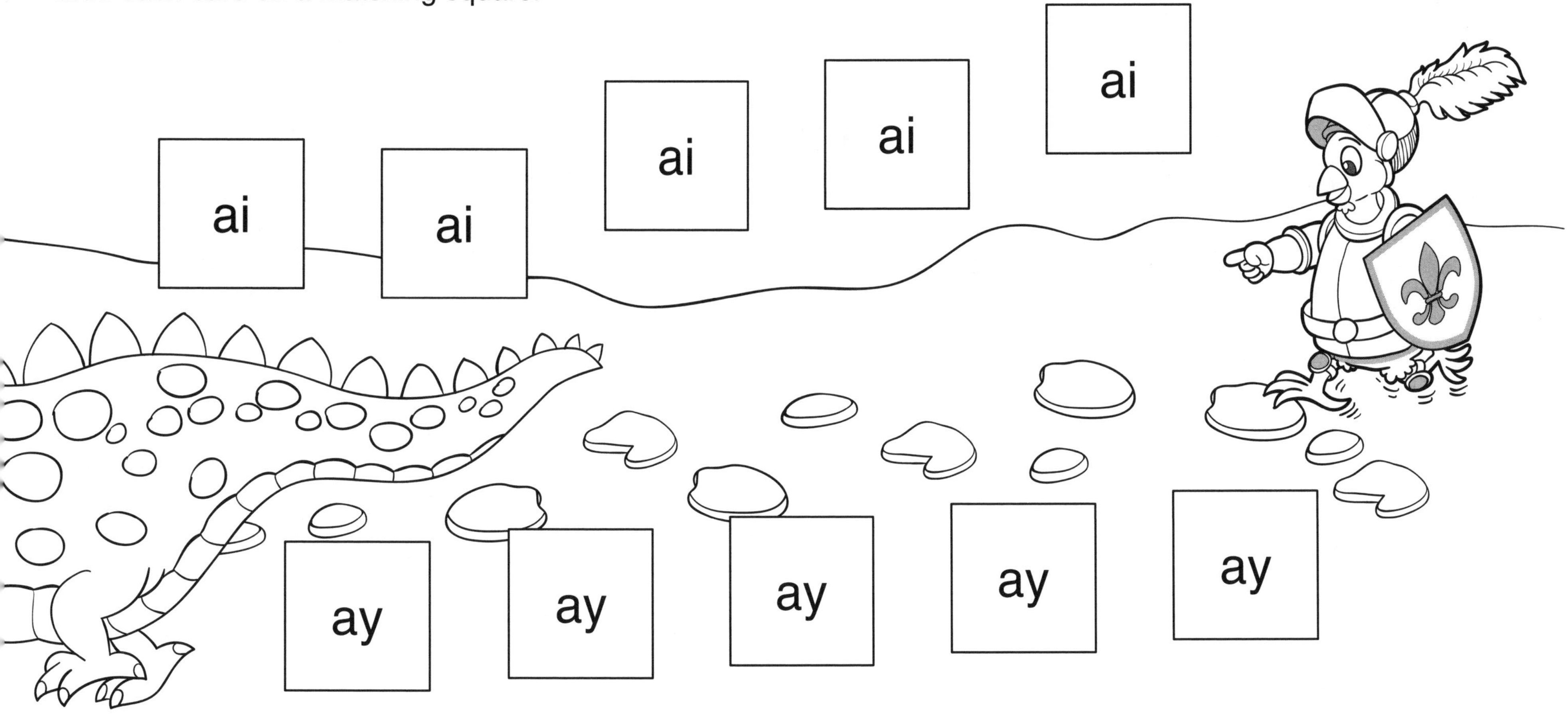

ai ai ai ai ai

ay ay ay ay ay

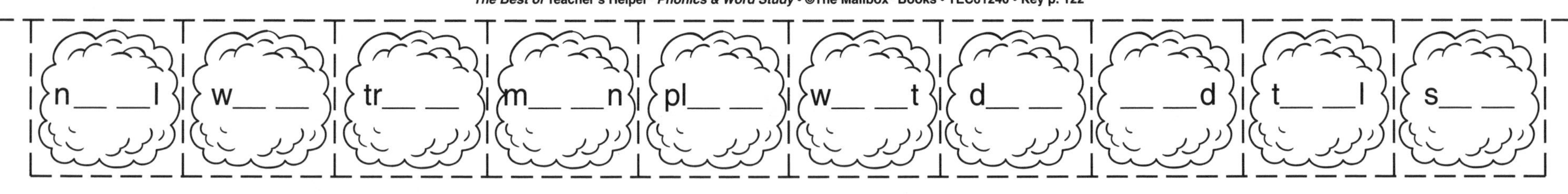
n__ __l
w__ __
tr__ __
m__ __n
pl__ __
w__ __t
d__ __
__ __d
t__ __l
s__ __

Name ______________________________

Shields for a Knight

Complete each word by writing *ea* or *ee.*
Color by the code.

Color Code
ea = yellow
ee = green
ch __ __ se
wh __ __ l
p __ __ ch
__ __ r
l __ __ f
f __ __ t
st __ __ m
j __ __ p
b __ __ d
qu __ __ n
t __ __ th
t __ __r
kn __ __
t __ __

Name ______________________________

Word Walls

Write each word on a brick on the correct tower.

oo **as in book**

oo **as in boot**

broom	cook
food	fool
foot	good
room	hoof
hook	pool
hood	look
mood	scoop
wool	moose
noon	stood
brook	loose

Bonus Box: On the back of this page, write at least two pairs of rhyming words that have *oo* in them. Use the words above to help you.

Name ____________________

Pretty Petals

Write *ai, ea,* or *oa* to complete the word on each petal.
Cut apart the petals.
Glue each one on the matching flower.

ea

ai

oa

Bonus Box: Write two more words that each contain *oa.*

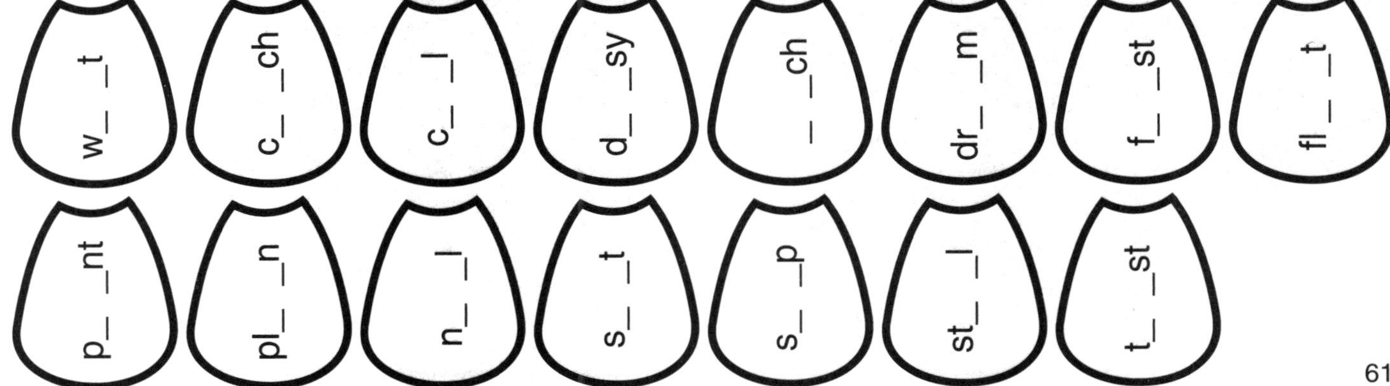
w__t
c__ch
c__l
d__sy
__ch
dr__m
f__st
fl__t
p__nt
pl__n
n__l
s__t
s__p
st__l
t__st

Name ______________________________

The One That Got Away!

Complete each word with *oi* or *oy*.
If you write *oi,* color the fish purple.
If you write *oy,* color the fish orange.

c __ __ n
enj __ __
t __ __ s
b __ __
r __ __ al
__ __ ly
c __ __ l
p __ __ nt
__ __ ster
destr __ __
Be careful! Make sure you've colored eight fish purple.
s __ __ l
b __ __ l
j __ __ ful
n __ __ sy
j __ __ nt
l __ __ al

Bonus Box: On the back of this page, write two more words that each contain *oi.*

Name ____________________

Hiking to the Top

Help Charlie and Chuck find the path to the top of the mountain.
If a word is spelled correctly, color the box green.
If a word is spelled incorrectly, write the correct spelling above the box.

brown
flower
trowt
power
cloud
mowse
houl
shout
owt
down
shower
sound
froun
house
sowr
pouder
croun
howr
proud
town
owl

Bonus Box: On the back of this page, write two more words that each contain *ou.*

Setting Up Camp

Read each clue.
Use the answers to complete the puzzle.
Hint: Each answer contains *oi, oy, ou,* or *ow.*

Across

3. a shellfish with a pearl inside
7. the taste of a lemon
8. if you're not quiet, you're ______
9. do this to water to make steam
10. yell or scream

Down

1. 60 minutes
2. the opposite of smile
4. a cloth used to dry things
5. the opposite of up
6. quarters, dimes, and nickels
9. a male child
11. an object to play with

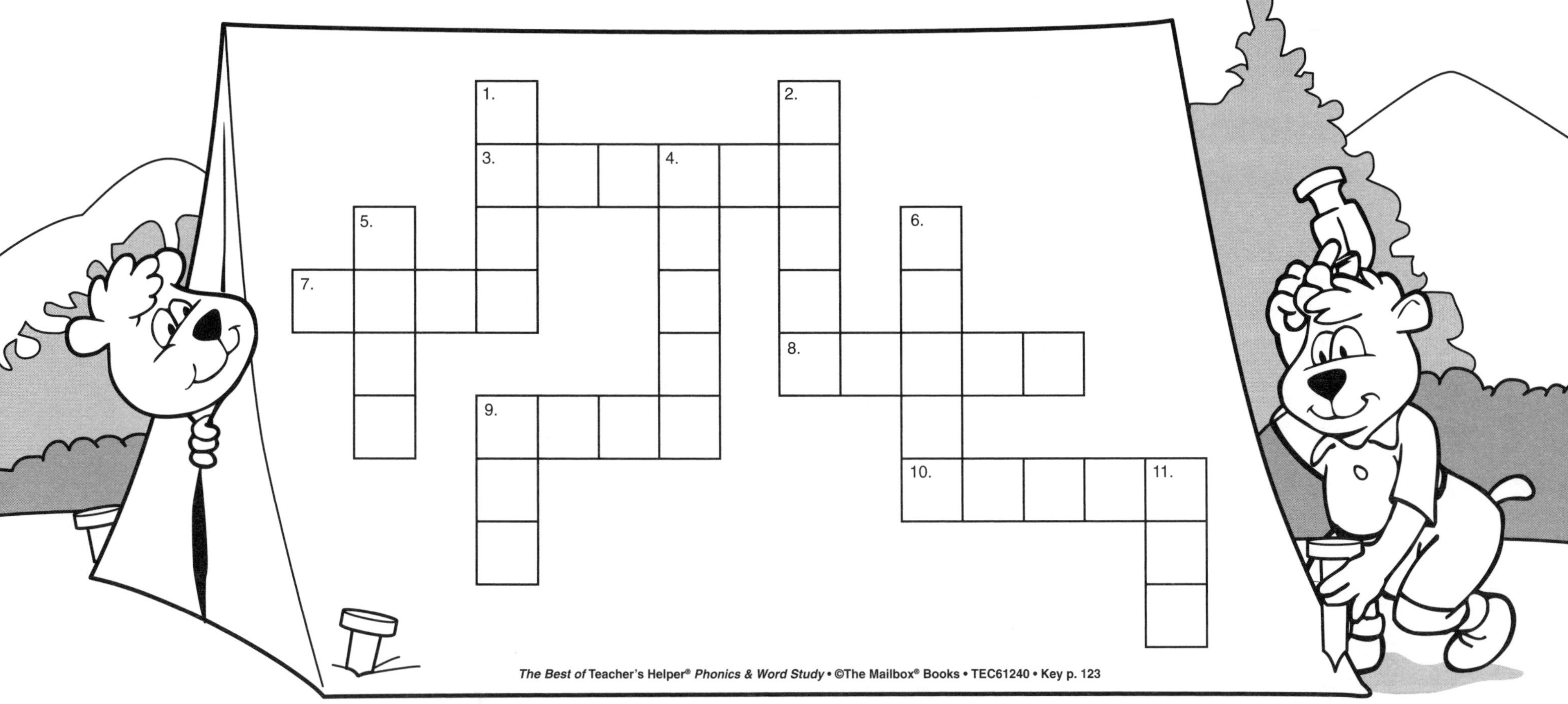
1.
2.
3.
4.
5.
6.
7.
8.
9.
10.
11.

Name ______________________________

Kicking Practice

Write *oi* or *oy* to complete each word.
Color by the code.

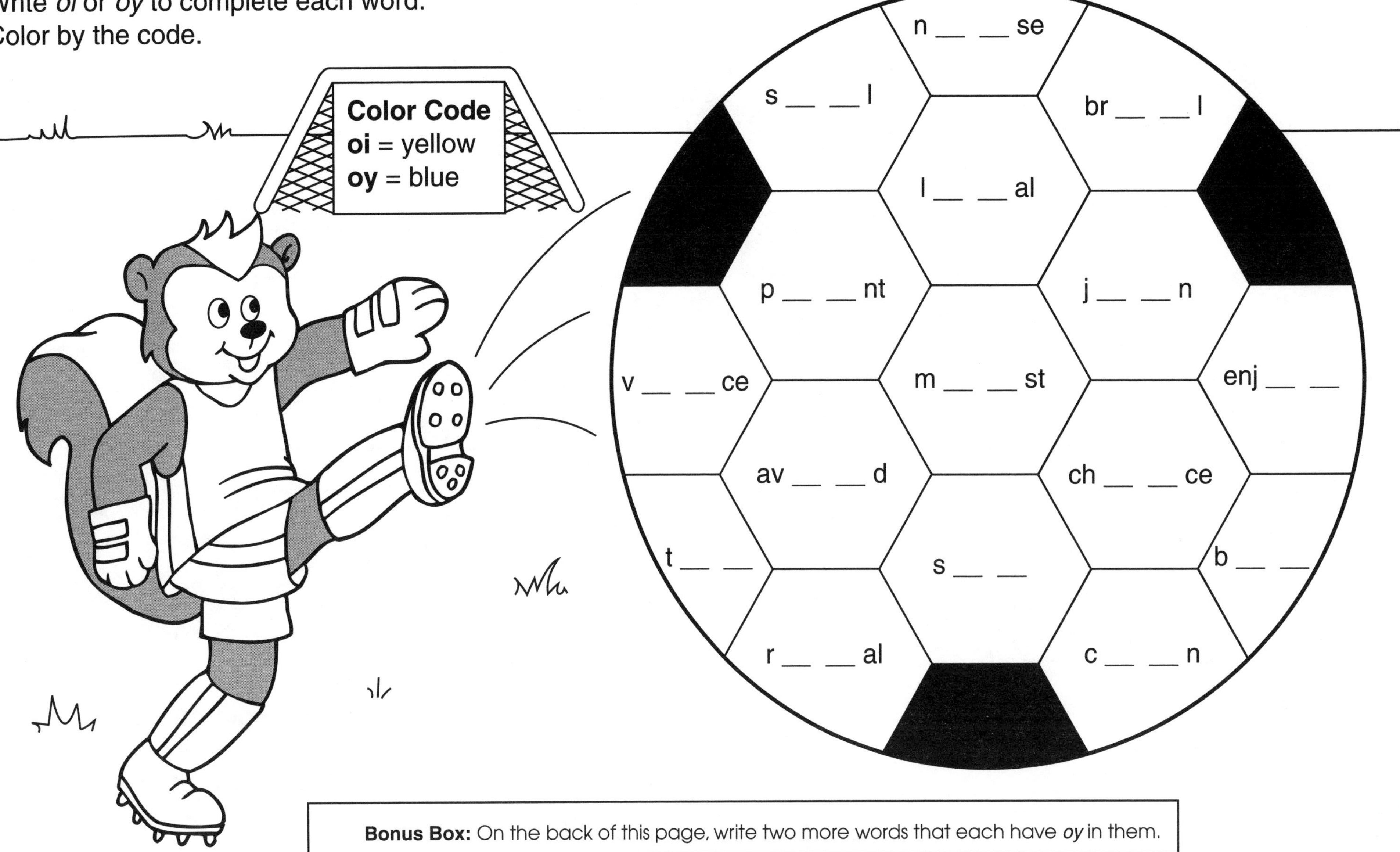
Color Code
oi = yellow
oy = blue
n __ __ se
s __ __ l
br __ __ l
l __ __ al
p __ __ nt
j __ __ n
v __ __ ce
m __ __ st
enj __ __
av __ __ d
ch __ __ ce
t __ __
s __ __
b __ __
r __ __ al
c __ __ n

Bonus Box: On the back of this page, write two more words that each have *oy* in them.

Name ______________________________

Warm-Up Relay

Write *ou* or *ow* to complete the word on each cone below.
Cut apart the cones.
Glue each one next to the matching ball.

ou

ow

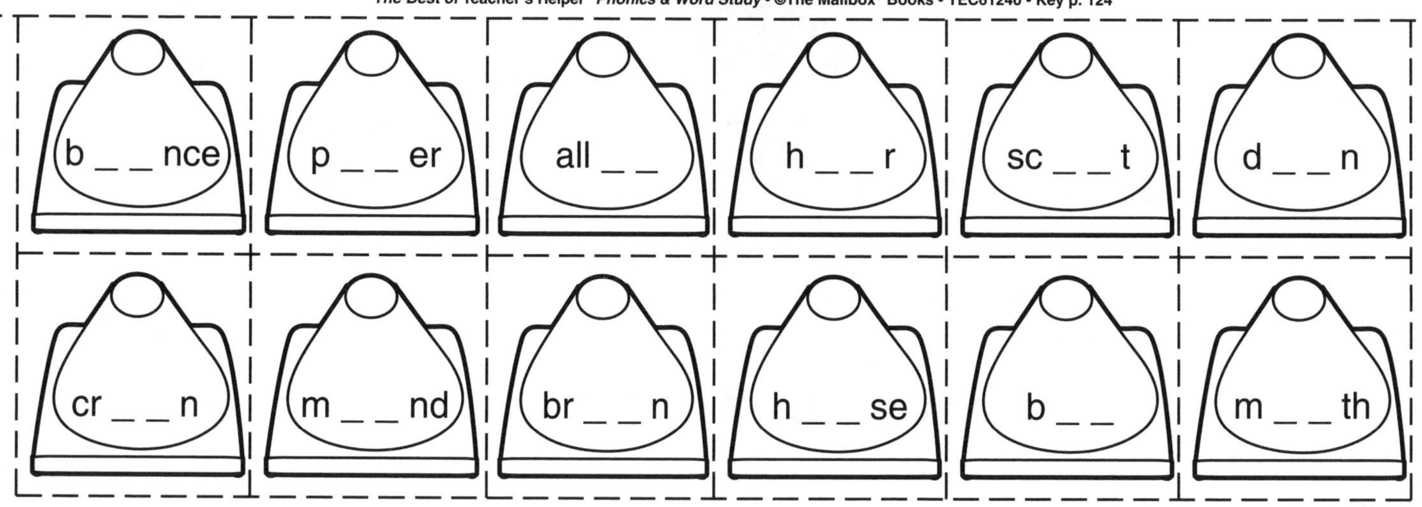
b _ _ nce
p _ _ er
all _ _
h _ _ r
sc _ _ t
d _ _ n
cr _ _ n
m _ _ nd
br _ _ n
h _ _ se
b _ _
m _ _ th

Name ____________________

Something Sweet

Write a word for each clue.
Color the word in the puzzle.

1. a cloth to dry with __ ow __ __

2. silly circus performers __ __ ow __ __
3. puffy white object in the sky __ __ ou __
4. a circle's shape __ ou __ __

5. the opposite of lost __ ou __ __
6. the opposite of up __ ow __
7. use this to talk __ ou __ __
8. object on a king's head __ __ ow __
9. the opposite of whisper __ __ ou __
10. a farm animal __ ow
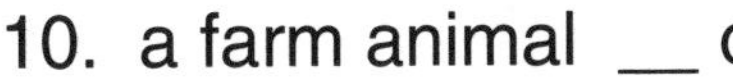
11. blooms in the spring __ __ ow __ __
12. said when someone is hurt ou __ __

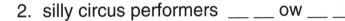

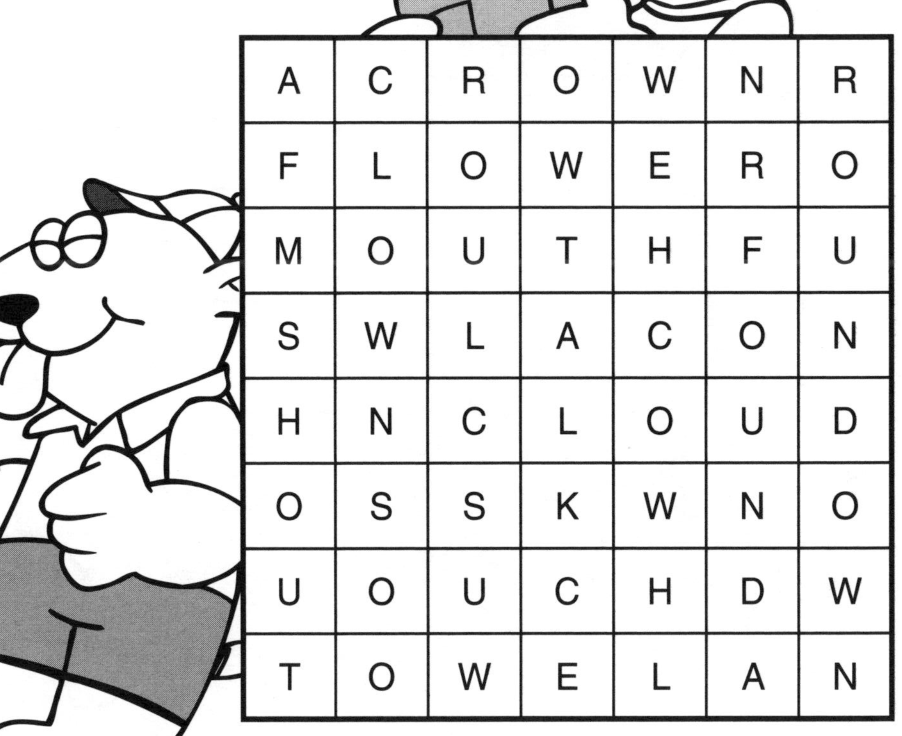
BEEP!
BEEP!
BEEP!
BLIP!

A	C	R	O	W	N	R
F	L	O	W	E	R	O
M	O	U	T	H	F	U
S	W	L	A	C	O	N
H	N	C	L	O	U	D
O	S	S	K	W	N	O
U	O	U	C	H	D	W
T	O	W	E	L	A	N

What is a polar bear's favorite dessert?
Arrange the uncolored puzzle letters on the lines below to solve the riddle.

Baked __ __ __ __ __ __

Name________________________________

Shells by the Shore

Complete each word by writing *oi* or *ow* on the lines.
Cut the word cards apart.
Glue each one on the matching pail.

oi
ow

Bonus Box: On the back of this sheet, write two more words that each have *ow* in them.

n___se	cr___n	c___n	gr___l	p___der	s___l
h___	p___nt	t___n	v___ce	sh___er	m___st

Name ______________________

Pack Rat Cats!

Write *ar* or *or* to complete each word.
Circle the words in the puzzle.

1. Cathy brought y __ __ n so she can knit between innings.
2. She wore her sc __ __ f and jacket.
3. Her __ __ m is broken, so she can't clap.
4. She will blow a h __ __ n to cheer for the team.
5. She brought popc __ __ n for a snack.
6. Cory's umbrella will protect him from a st __ __ m.
7. He eats peanuts from a j __ __.
8. He brought tweezers in case he gets a th __ __ n.
9. He hopes a st __ __ player will sign his baseball.
10. Where will Cory and Cathy park their c __ __ t?

M
CATS
MUD
g s h i r t h o r n
v c o p o p c o r n
r a r m s l a t a l
h r n x j a r f s m
u f o b y t t e t f
n p j r c z d o a w
y a r n k s t o r m

Bonus Box: On the back of this sheet, write three more words that each have *or* in them.

Name ____________________

Catch!

Write *er* or *ir* to complete each word.
Color by the code.

Color Code
er = blue
ir = yellow

b __ __ d

f __ __ n

c __ __ cus

aft __ __

g __ __ l

st __ __

d __ __ t

p __ __ son

p __ __ ky

sk __ __ t

tw __ __ l

j __ __ k

MUDCATS

MUD

Bonus Box: Circle each word that is spelled correctly.
therd mercy ferst thirty

The Best of Teacher's Helper® *Phonics & Word Study* • ©The Mailbox® Books • TEC61240 • Key p. 124

Name ______________________________

Something Smells Good!

Write *er* or *ur* to complete each word in the boxes below.
Cut apart the boxes.
Put a dot of glue on each •.
Glue each box on the matching clue.

COTTON CANDY $1.00

• to pull sharply	• an animal with a shell	• a tiny insect	• what a bear has	• a place where money is kept
• the opposite of before	• a place where a bird sits	• a mixture of red and blue	• injured	• to rush

Bonus Box: On the back of this sheet, write three more words that each have *ur* in them.

j _ _ k	h_ _ry	t _ _ mite	p_ _se	f_ _
aft_ _	p _ _ ple	t_ _tle	h_ _ t	p_ _ch

Time for the Game!

Circle the letter for the word that completes each sentence.

MUDCATS
MUDCATS
MUD

1. Cathy and Cory love watching _____.
   e. sports   m. sparts
2. But they _____ to watch baseball.
   s. prefir   y. prefer
3. They ride the bus to the _____.
   g. pirk   f. park
4. Cory wears his team _____.
   h. jursey   s. jersey
5. Cathy wears her favorite _____.
   v. shirt   t. shert
6. It's _____, just like the team's caps.
   l. perple   t. purple
7. They cheer for the _____ baseman.
   n. first   b. furst
8. He is the _____ of the team.
   e. stur   i. star
9. He _____ lots of points!
   p. scures   r. scores
10. They hope he'll have a _____ game!
    a. perfect   o. purfect

Why is the baseball park so cool?

To solve the riddle, match the circled letters above to the numbered lines below.

Because there's a __ __ __ (3 10 7) __ __ (8 7) __ __ __ __ __ (1 5 1 9 2) __ __ __ __ (4 1 10 6)!

Name____________________

Word Hurdles

Help Francine Frog jump the hurdles!
Write **ar** or **er** to complete each word.

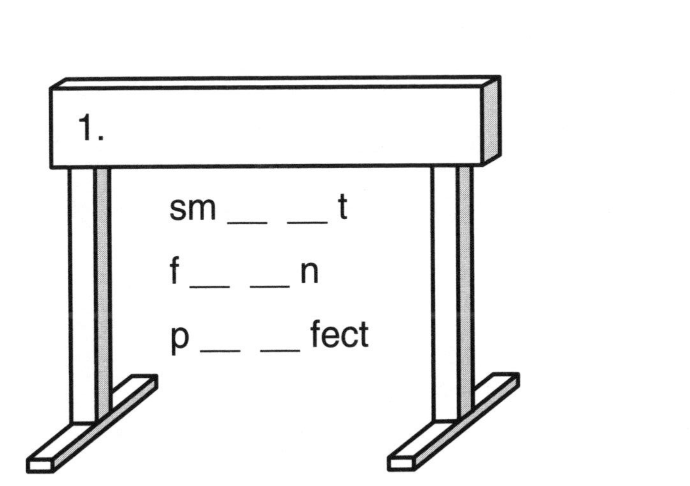

1.
sm __ __ t
f __ __ n
p __ __ fect

2.
c __ __ tain
f __ __ mer
lett __ __

3.
b __ __ n
p __ __ ty
h __ __ self

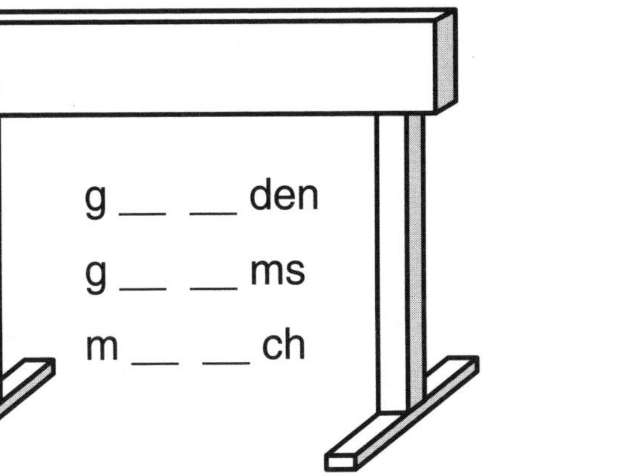

4.
g __ __ den
g __ __ ms
m __ __ ch

5.
n __ __ ve
st __ __ n
ch __ __ t

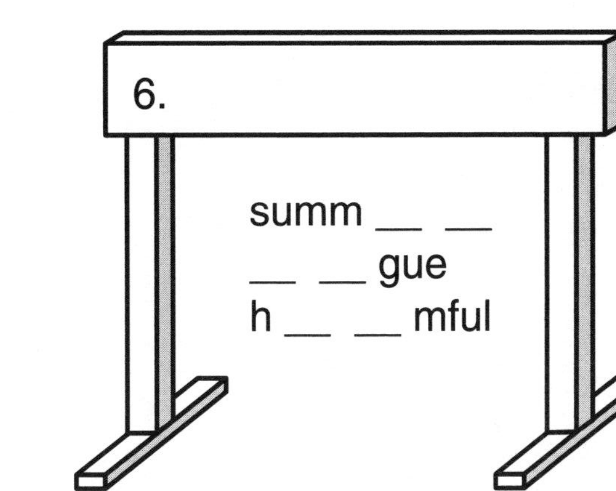

6.
summ __ __
__ __ gue
h __ __ mful

Bonus Box: On the back of this page, write three sentences. Use at least one word from the hurdles above in each sentence.

Name____________________

Lengthy Leaping

Read each clue.
Write the word that answers the clue.
Hint: Each word contains *ir* or *or*.

1. the opposite of boy (_) _ _ _
2. the center of an apple _ _ _ (_)
3. the prickly part of a rose _ _ _ _ (_)
4. a make-believe horse with one horn (_) _ _ _ _ _ _
5. a bird's sound _ _ _ _ (_)
6. a round shape _ _ _ _ (_) _
7. not clean _ _ (_) _ _
8. to mix with a spoon (_) _ _ _
9. the opposite of less (_) _ _ _
10. not exciting _ (_) _ _ _ _

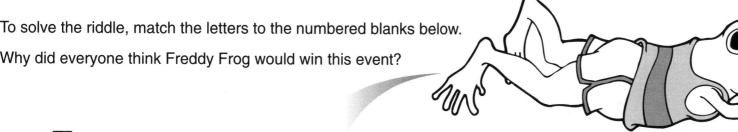

To solve the riddle, match the letters to the numbered blanks below.

Why did everyone think Freddy Frog would win this event?

He comes from a whole family of

_ _ _ _ J _ _ _ _ _ _ !
6 10 3 1   4 9 5 2 7 8

Bonus Box: On the back of this page, write two more words that each contain *ir*. Then write two more words that each contain *or*.

Name ____________________

R-Controlled Vowels
Spelling review

Up and Over

Unscramble each set of letters to form a word with *ar, ir, er,* or *or.* Write the word on the line across from each set of letters.

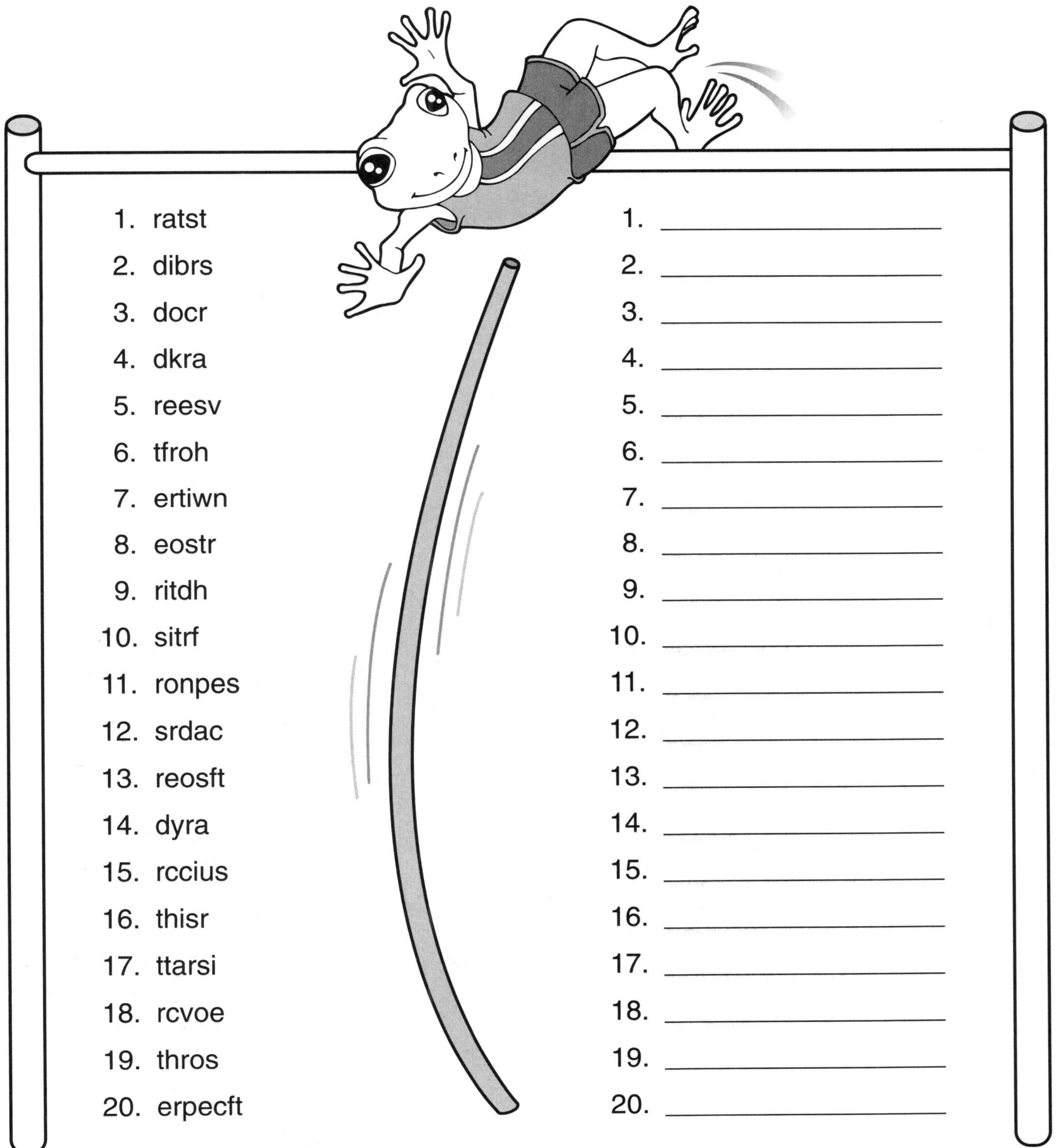

1. ratst
2. dibrs
3. docr
4. dkra
5. reesv
6. tfroh
7. ertiwn
8. eostr
9. ritdh
10. sitrf
11. ronpes
12. srdac
13. reosft
14. dyra
15. rccius
16. thisr
17. ttarsi
18. rcvoe
19. thros
20. erpecft

Bonus Box: Choose ten words from this list. On the back of this sheet, write the words in alphabetical order.

Name________________________________

Top Ten Songs

Write *ar* or *ir* to complete each word.

1. "Running in C__ __cles"
2. "I've Come So F__ __ to Be a St__ __"
3. "B__ __ds in the G__ __den"
4. "Time to St__ __t the P__ __ty"
5. "The Th__ __d Monday in M__ __ch"
6. "St__ __ Things Up, S__ __!"
7. "G__ __l With a Polka-Dot Sk__ __t"
8. "It's D__ __k at the M__ __ket Tonight"
9. "H__ __d to Always Go F__ __st"
10. "Th__ __ty D__ __ty Pairs of Shoes"

Bonus Box: Color the musical notes above.
Color by the code.
Added *ar* to the title = red
Added *ir* to the title = yellow
Added *ar* and *ir* to the title = orange

Name ________________________________

A Rave Review

Circle each misspelled word.

Entertainment News

Concirt Review
by G. Girbil

If you haven't seen the Traveling Trio, you're missing a real treat! Hirman, Howie, and Hurbie Hamstir are turrific! Last night, they pirformed in New Jursey. Evury pirson who saw them was thrilled. If you want to see a purfect show, buy a ticket! I'm cirtain you'll love it.

Write each circled word correctly on the lines below.

☆ ____________ 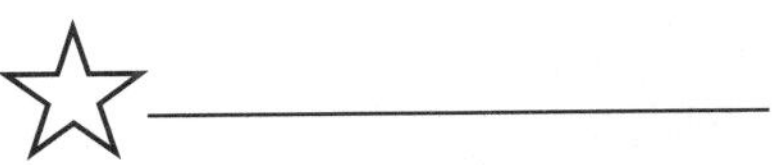 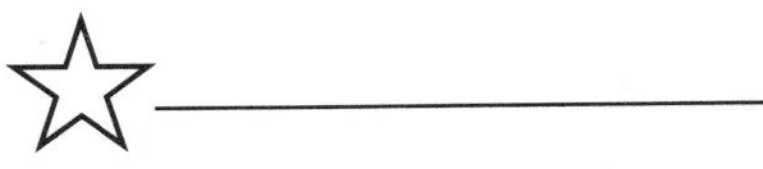

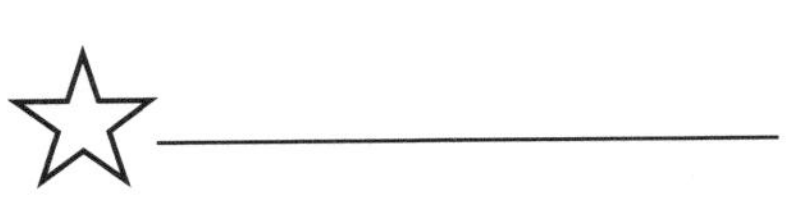 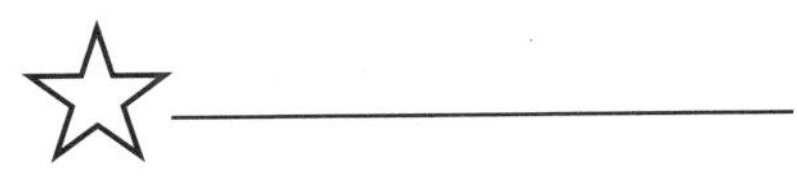 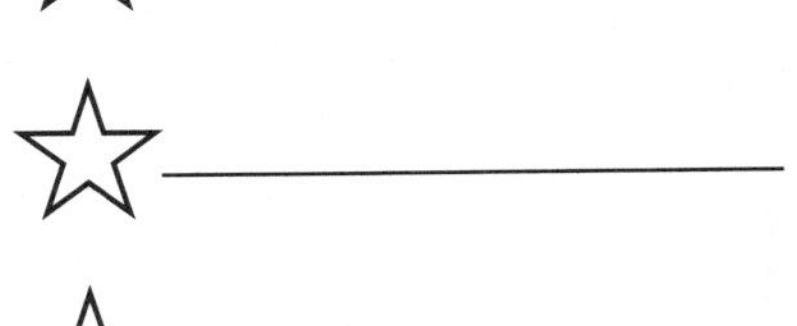

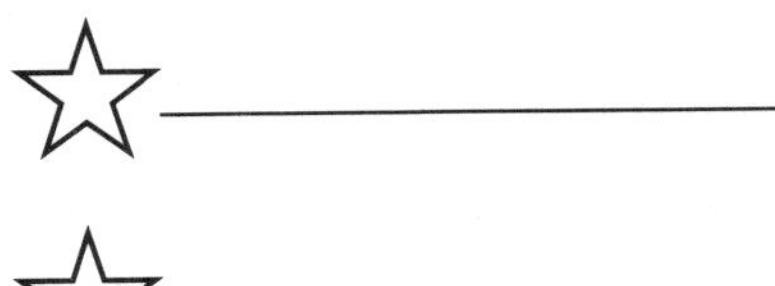 ☆ ____________ ☆ ____________

☆ ____________ ☆ ____________ ☆ ____________

Name____

Baking Cookies

Look at each word.
If it has a soft *g* sound, write it on one of Gina's cookies.
If it has a hard *g* sound, write it on one of Gary's cookies.

gym	gobble
giant	gem
gum	gentle
golf	gypsy
gain	gave

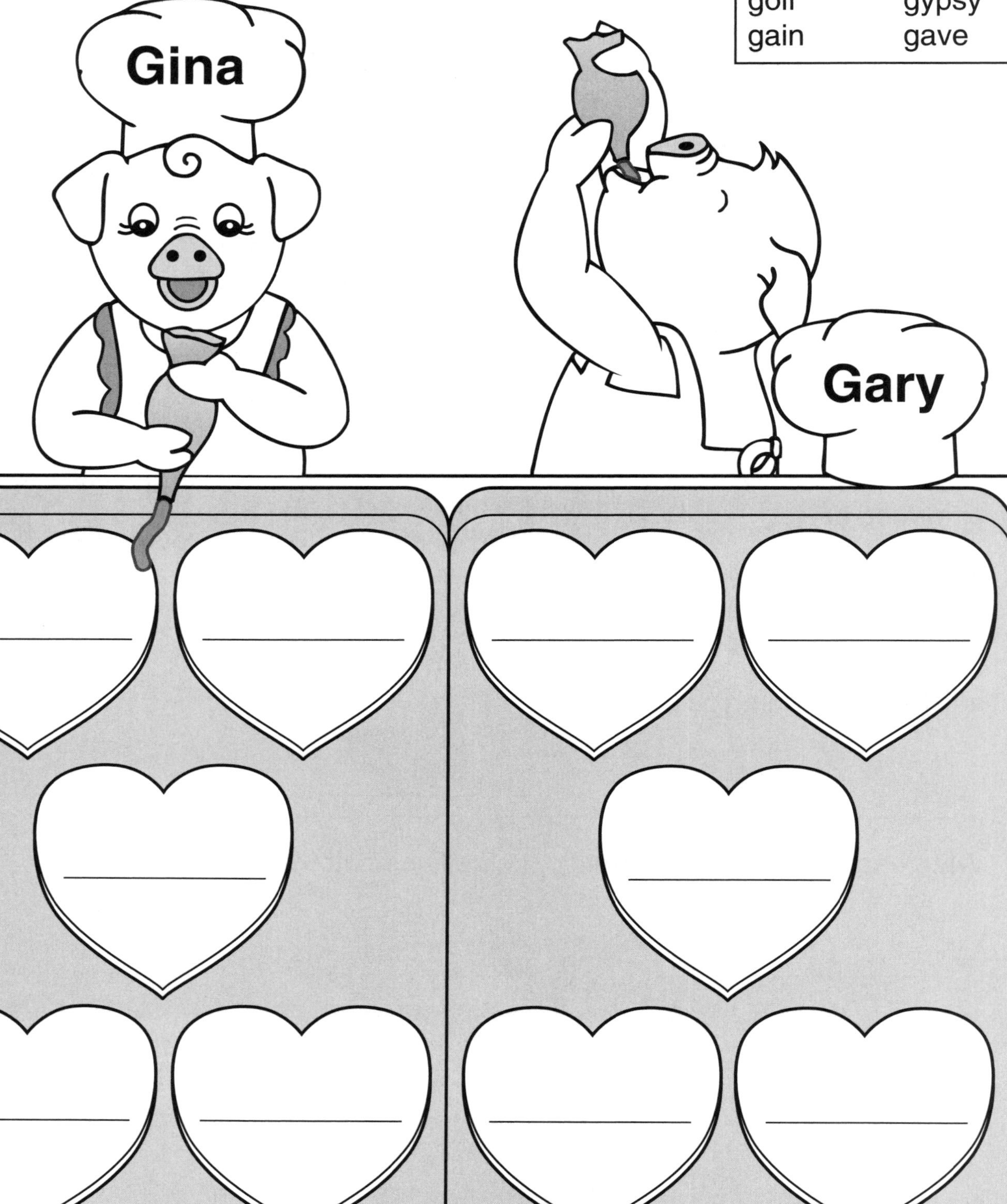
Gina
Gary

Name ____________________

Pouring Cups of Tea

Color by the code.

Color Code
soft *c* = purple
hard *c* = red

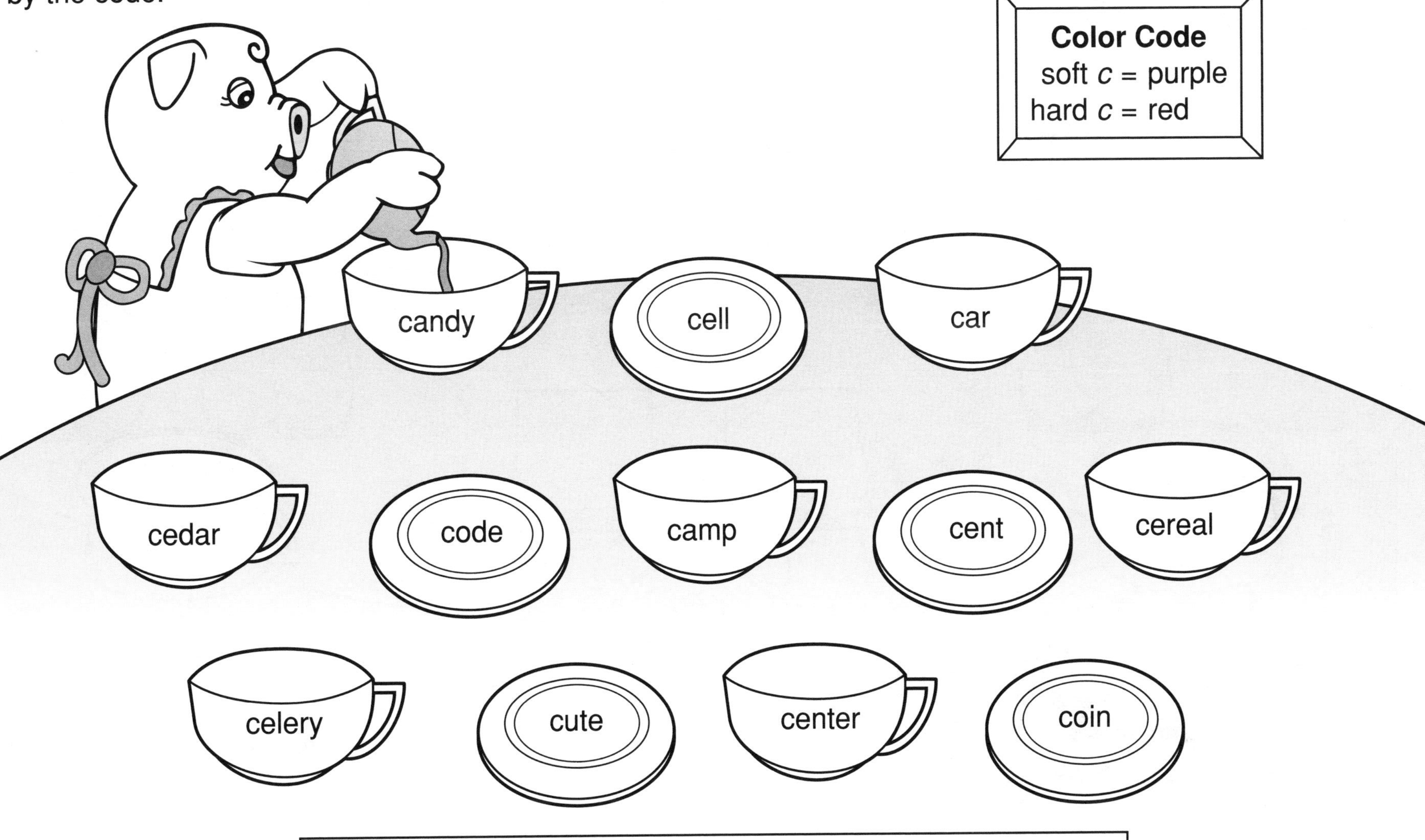
candy
cell
car
cedar
code
camp
cent
cereal
celery
cute
center
coin

Bonus Box: Write a word that has a soft *c* sound and hard *c* sound. Use the picture to the right to help you. ____________________

Name ____________________

Time for Tea

Cut out the cookies below.
Find the teacup with letters that complete the words on each cookie.
Glue each cookie into place.
Write the new words on the lines.

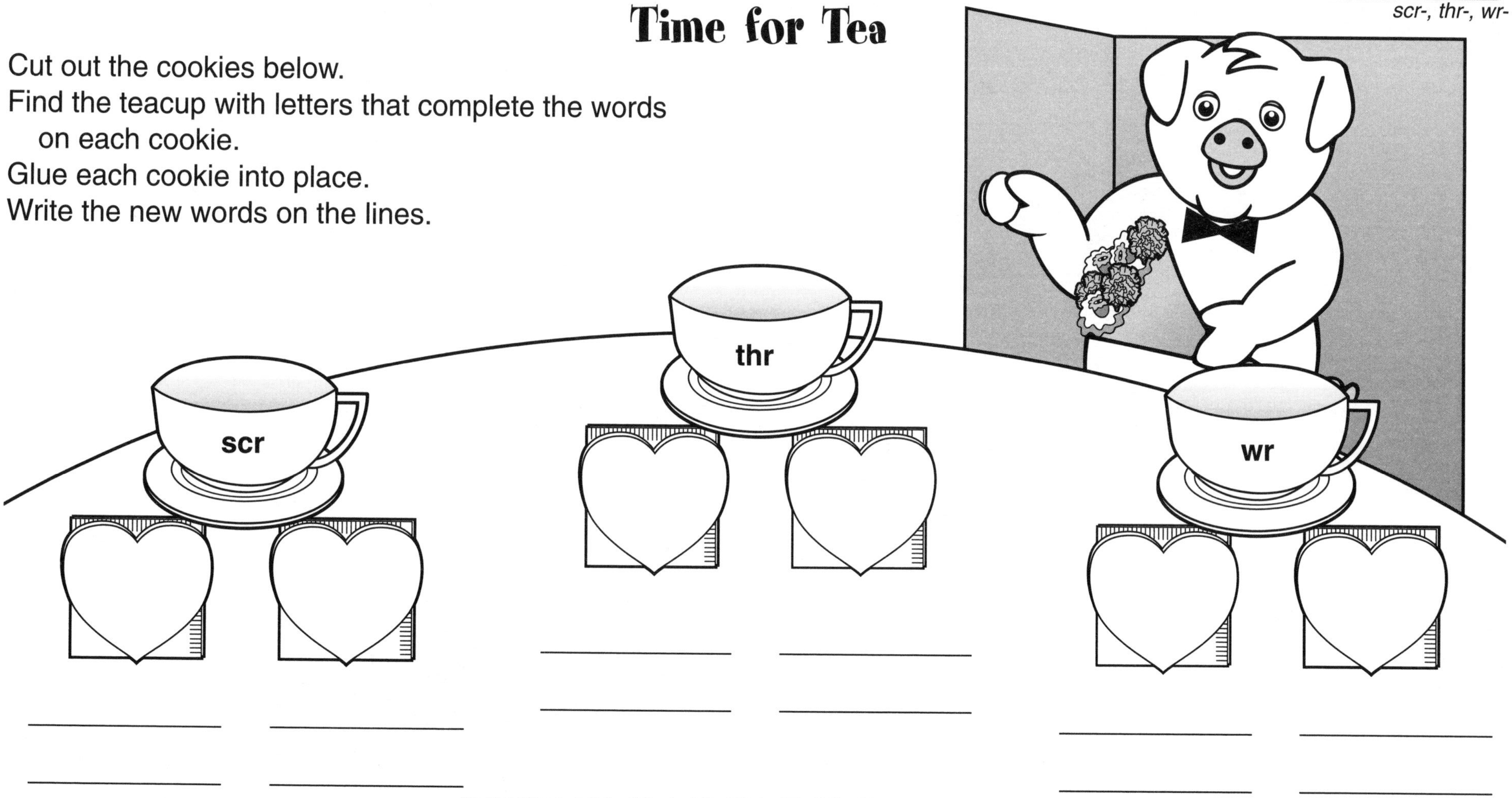

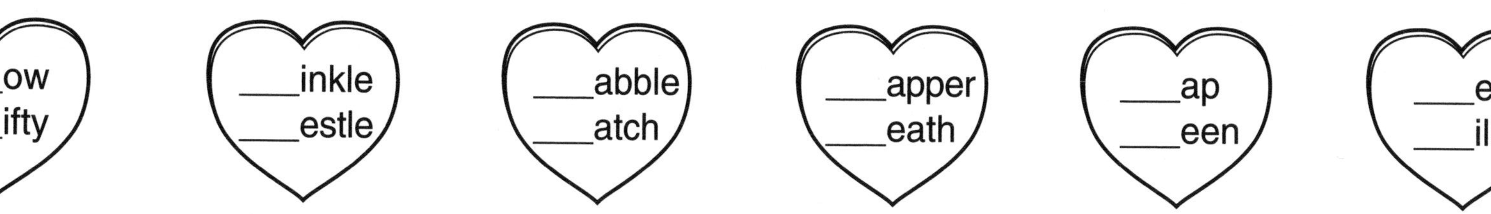
scr
thr
wr

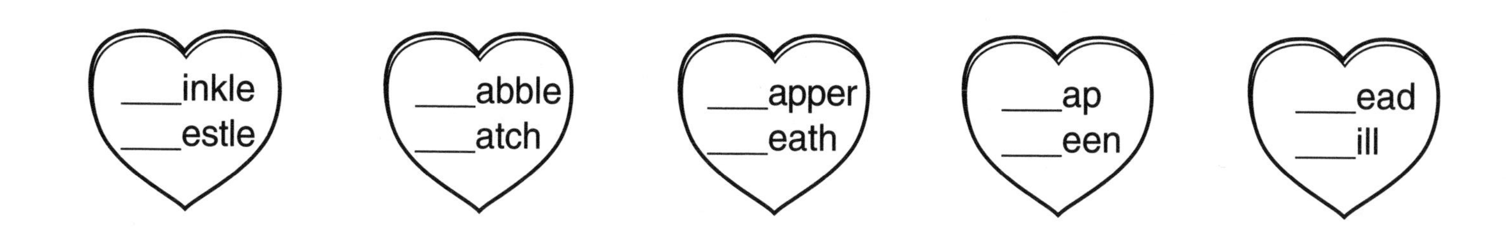

___ow	___inkle	___abble	___apper	___ap	___ead
___ifty	___estle	___atch	___eath	___een	___ill

Name____ Complex Consonants
-ch, -ck, -tch

Washing Tons of Teapots

Write *ch, ck,* or *tch* to complete each word.

1. pea_______
2. tru_______
3. wa_______
4. de_______
5. ea_______
6. no_______
7. tri_______
8. stre_______
9. whi_______
10. tou_______
11. fe_______
12. clo_______

Bonus Box: Write *ch, ck,* or *tch* to complete each word in the sentences. We go to the bea_____ and walk on the do_____. Then we eat crun_____y sna_____s while we wa_____ the swimmers.

Name ____ Complex Consonants
-ch, -tch

Green Thumb?

Complete each word by writing *ch* or *tch* on the lines.
Color the leaves by the code.

1 Leo and Lily are planting a vegetable pa________.

2 Leo leaves an in________ between his seeds.

3 Lily spaces her seeds mu________ farther apart.

4 The friends cover each seed with a pin________ of dirt.

5 Then they water, wa________, and wait.

6 They wonder whi________ seeds will sprout first.

7 Soon Lily says, "Leo, I have su________ good news for you!"

8 "Your plants are growing, but mine aren't," she says. "Will you swi________?"

9 "Don't tou________ that!" Leo warns.

10 "Why not?" Lily asks, about to rea________ out.

11 "It will make you i________!" says Leo.

12 "It's not my spina________," he cries. "It's poison ivy!"

Color Code
added *ch* = green
added *tch* = yellow

Name________________________________

Up, Up, and Away!

Read the word on each window.
If the word is a compound word, color the window yellow.
If the word is not a compound word, color the window black.

homework	bicycle
lighthouse	footprint
musical	bedroom

afternoon	review
cupcake	notebook

mailbox	inside
safety	daylight
earring	telephone
goldfish	slowly

Bonus Box: On the back of this sheet, list three compound words that each contain the word *some*.

Name ______________________________

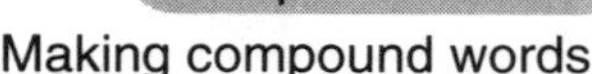
Compound Words

Making compound words

Super Strength

Cut out the circles below.
Glue each circle on a barbell to make a compound word.
Write the word on the line below the barbell.

1.

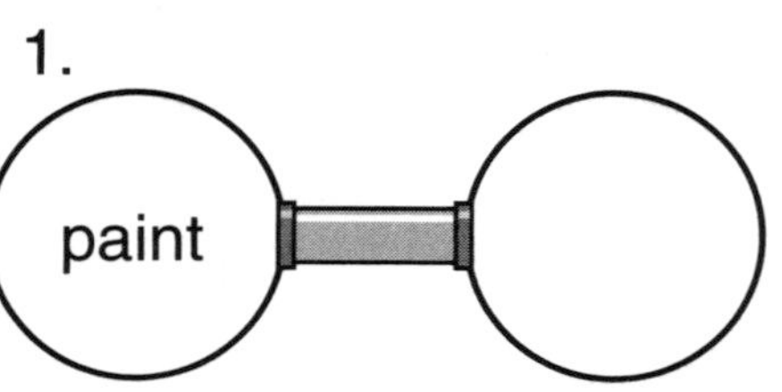
paint

____

2.

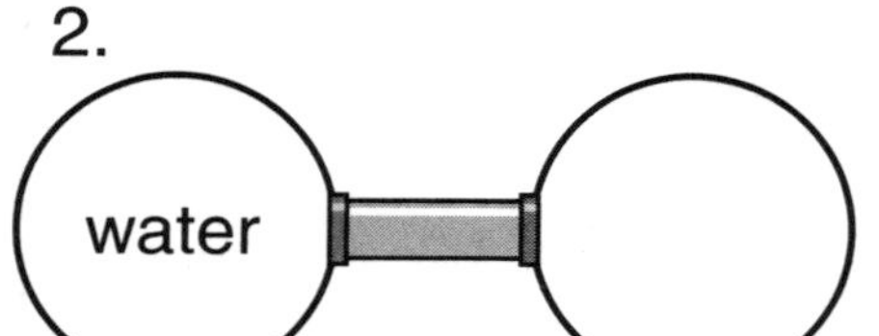
water

____

3.

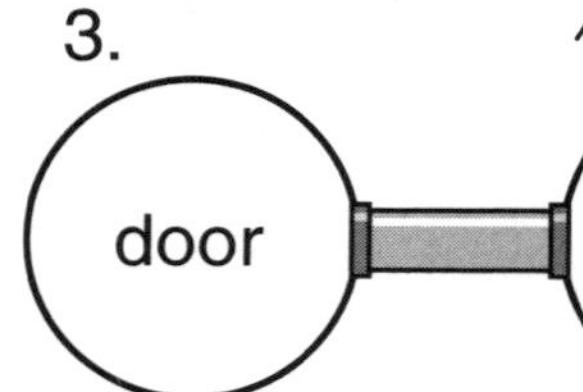
door

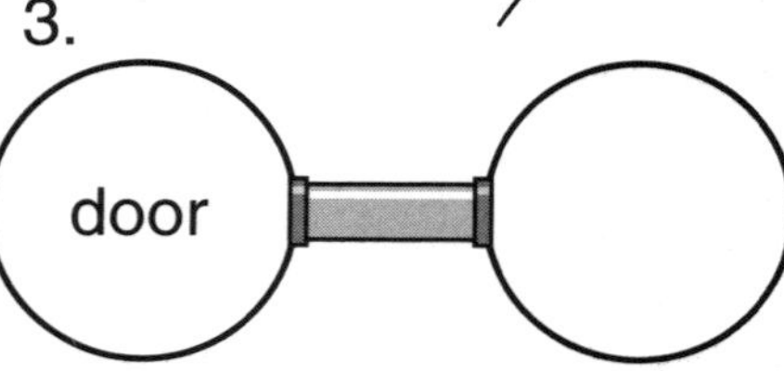

____

4.

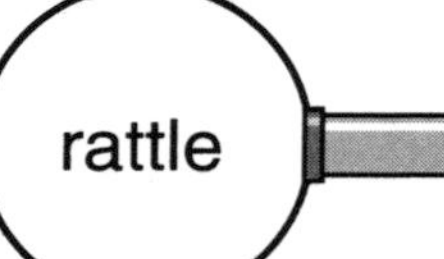
rattle

____

5.

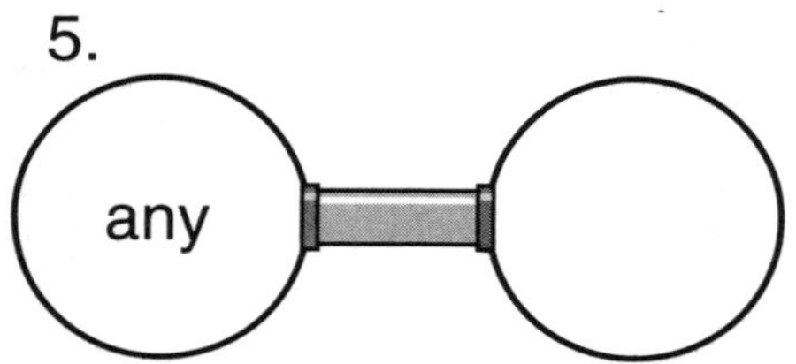
any

____

6.

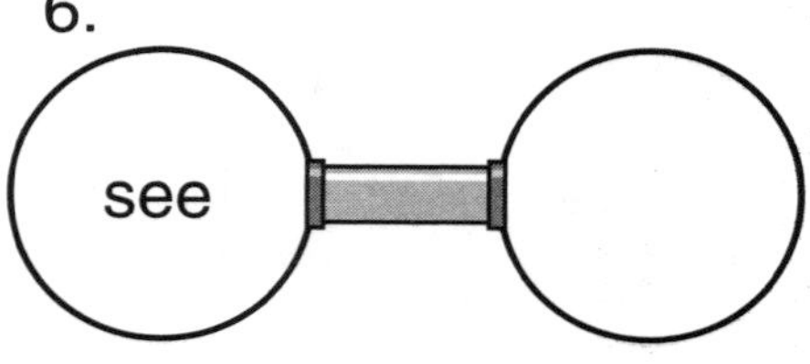
see

____

7.

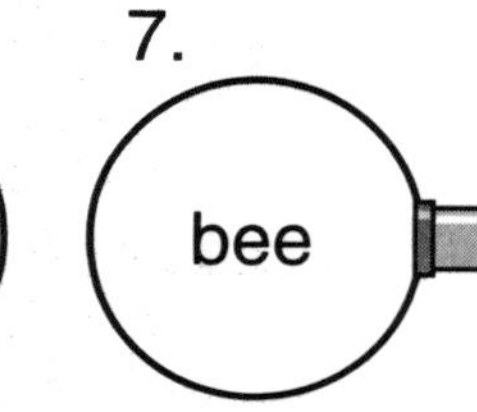
bee

____

8.

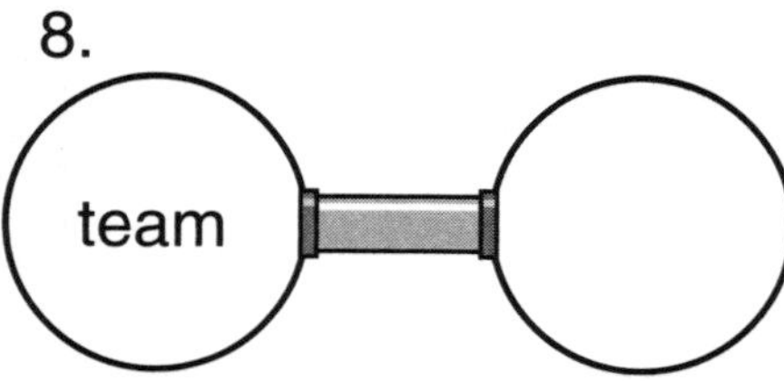
team

____

9.

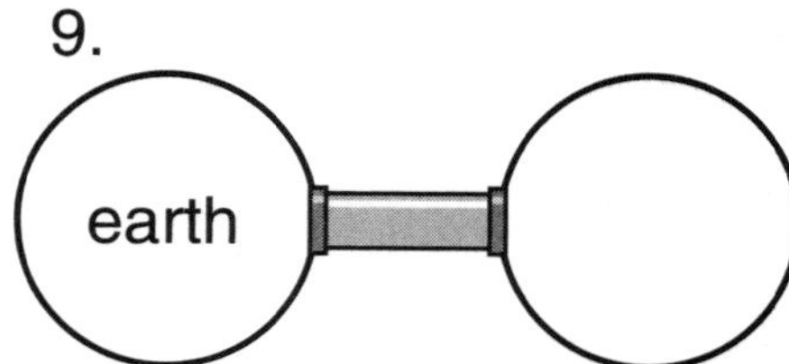
earth

____

10.

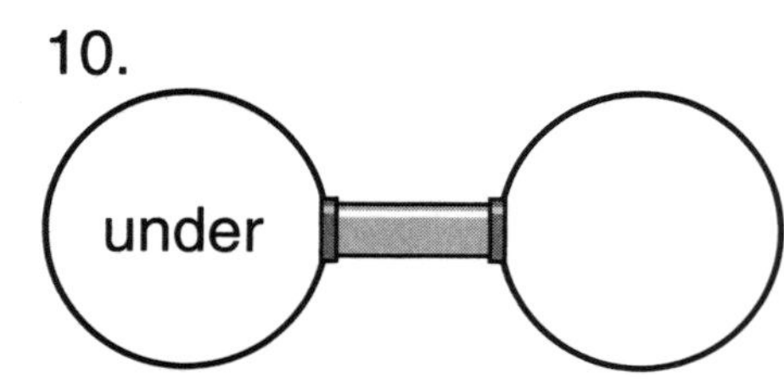
under

____

The Best of Teacher's Helper® *Phonics & Word Study* • ©The Mailbox® Books • TEC61240 • Key p. 125

hive work melon brush quake

stand snake where saw bell

Name ______________________________

A True Hero

Draw lines to make compound words.

SUPER ELEPHANT SAVES THE DAY!

SE
WAREHOUSE

Every •	• head
head •	• house
news •	• lines
over •	• one
ware •	• paper

air •	• end
fire •	• fall
them •	• fighters
water •	• plane
week •	• selves

Use the new words to complete the story.

Pick up a ______________! Read the ______________! Last ______________, there was a big fire. An empty ______________ was burning. The ______________ were the first to arrive. They could not put out the fire by ______________. Then they saw something flying ______________! It wasn't an ______________. It was an elephant! He sprayed a ______________ from his trunk. ______________ agrees that this elephant is a hero!

Name ___________________________

Scrambled Acorns

Match each top word with one bottom word to make a compound word.
The first one has been done for you.

1.
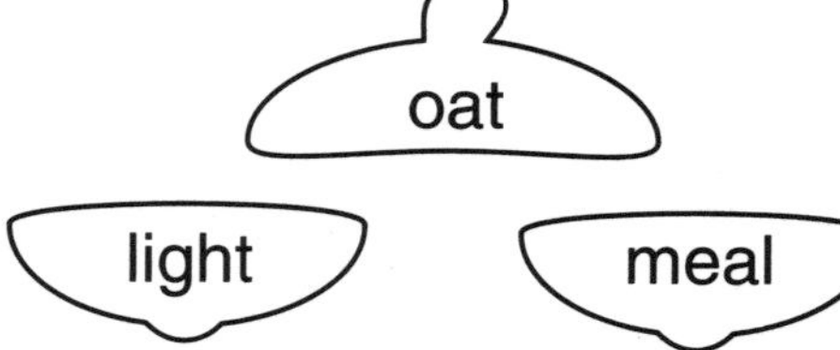
oat
light
meal

oatmeal

5.

under
north
ground

____

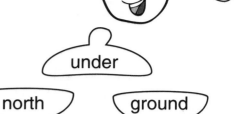

2.
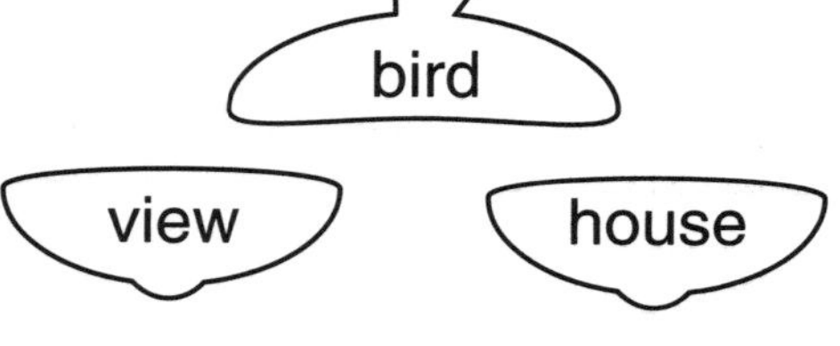
bird
view
house

____

6.
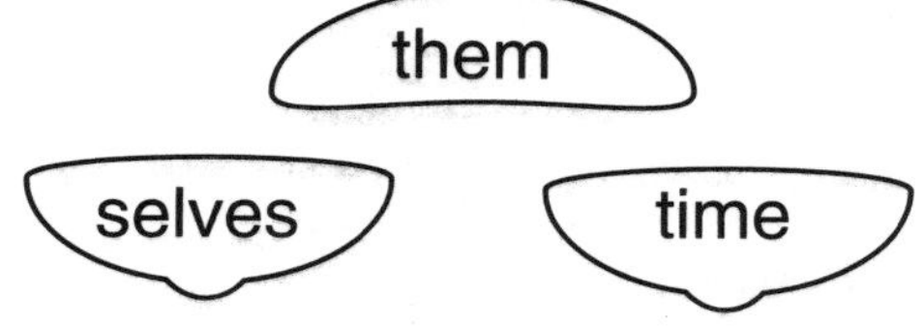
them
selves
time

____

3.
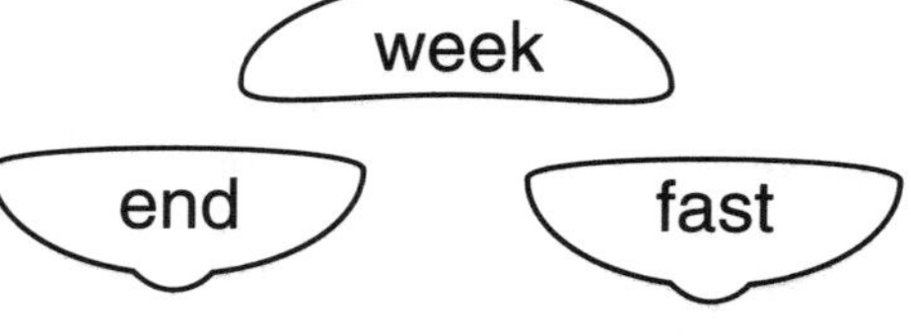
week
end
fast

____

7.
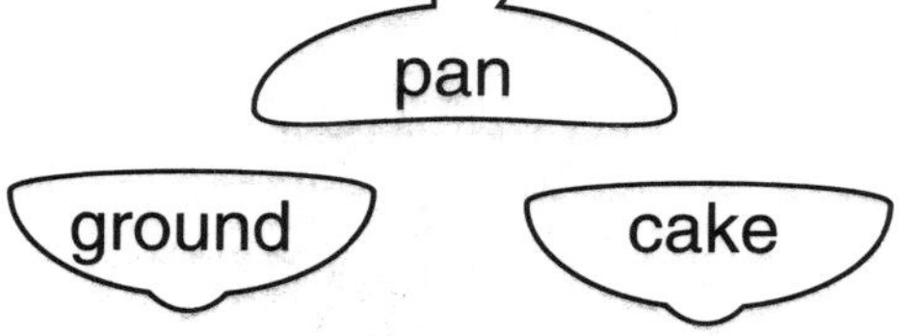
pan
ground
cake

____

4.
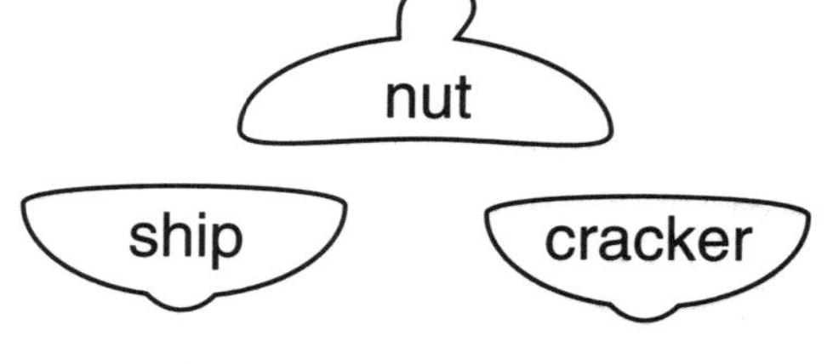
nut
ship
cracker

____

8.
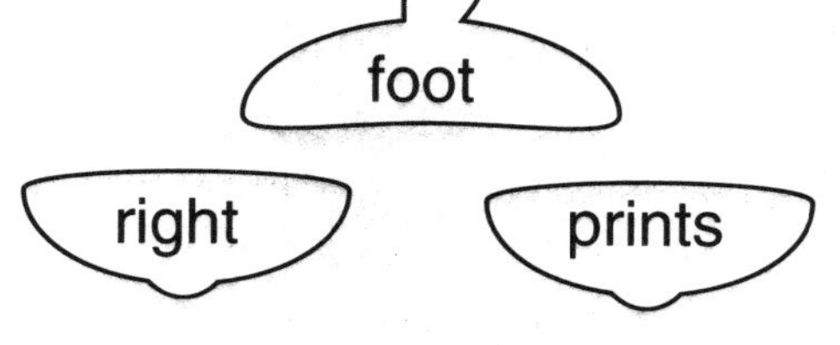
foot
right
prints

____

Write a word that completes each sentence.
Use the compound words from above.

1. Squirrel gathers acorns and hides them ______________.
2. He covers his ______________ so no one will find the hiding place.
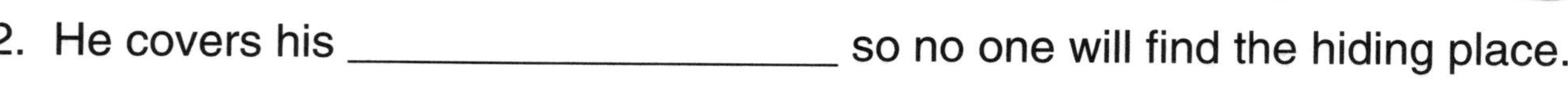
3. He would rather eat acorns than a bowl of ______________.
4. Squirrel loves to gather acorns on cold ______________ days.

Name ______________________________

By the Birdhouses

Make a compound word by adding each word on the first birdhouse to a word on the second birdhouse.

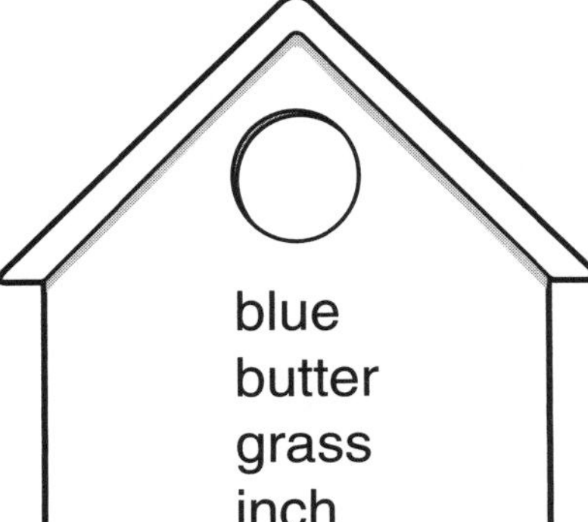

First birdhouse		Second birdhouse
blue	1. ______	tops
butter	2. ______	flies
grass	3. ______	side
inch	4. ______	be
may	5. ______	worm
rain	6. ______	birds
out	7. ______	hopper
spring	8. ______	drops
sun	9. ______	time
tree	10. ______	flowers

Use the compound words to complete the poem.

In the Backyard

Look closely and ______ you will see
A small ______ or a buzzing bee.
Feathery ______ sing songs for hours,
And tiny seeds become ______.
Green leaves appear on high ______,
And gray clouds send down small ______.
A ______ might go jumping by,
Or ______ may glide through the sky.
Yes, ______ days are filled with fun
And playing ______ in the warm, bright sun.

Bonus Box: *Butterfly* and *grasshopper* are compound words. Name another insect with a name that is a compound word.

Name ____________________

Teamwork

Identifying contractions

If the boxed word is a contraction, color it yellow.
If the boxed word is not a contraction, color it red.

Mia Mole's favorite [video] game is "Underground Adventure." [She's] a very good player, but she [doesn't] like to play alone. She often [asks] her brother Marco to join her. Then [he'll] play too. Mia and Marco [want] to win the game. [They'll] travel through the [tunnels] together. They [won't] stop until they succeed. Mia is best at digging holes. And Marco? [He's] a great treasure finder! [It's] [lots] of fun for them to play together. [They're] a great team!

Write each contraction from above on the lines below.
Then write the two words that make up each contraction.
The first one has been done for you.

1. She's = She + is
2. ________ = ________ + ________
3. ________ = ________ + ________
4. ________ = ________ + ________
5. ________ = ________ + ________
6. ________ = ________ + ________
7. ________ = ________ + ________
8. ________ = ________ + ________

Underground Adventure

Bonus Box: On the back of this page, write three sentences about video games. Use a different contraction in each sentence.

Name ____________________

Mole Vs. Mole

Combining words to form contractions

Combine the words on the chairs to make contractions.
Write the contractions on the screen.
Some words will be used more than once.

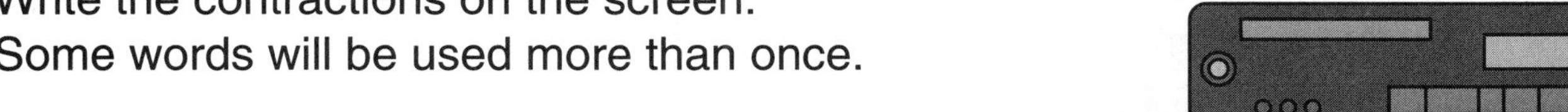

________	________	________	________
________	________	________	________
________	________	________	________
________	________	________	________
________	________	________	________

I
will
he
is
it
do
they

are
you
not
she
have
does

Name ________________________________

Game Over

Cut apart the squares below.
Find the squares with contractions that are spelled correctly.
Glue each one on the matching square on the screen.

you will
I am
are not
we are
they have
will not
it is
he had
I have
she is
did not
they are

arn't	its	I'm	I'v	won't	youl'l	he'ed	I've
didn't	we're	you'll	they're	they'ave	I'am	di'dnt	sh'es
he'd	she's	they've	we'er	the'yre	it's	aren't	willn't

Name ______________________________

Words that form contractions

Bow Ties for Dad

Write the two words that form each contraction on the lines below.

1. we'll

3. I'm

2. he's

4. don't

6. isn't

5. we're

9. they're

7. aren't

8. I'll

13. they've

11. it's

10. you've

12. can't

14. won't

1. ______________________
2. ______________________
3. ______________________
4. ______________________
5. ______________________
6. ______________________
7. ______________________
8. ______________________
9. ______________________
10. ______________________
11. ______________________
12. ______________________
13. ______________________
14. ______________________

Bonus Box: *Can't* and *don't* are both contractions that are formed with the word *not* and another word. On the back of this sheet, write two other words that are each formed with the word *not* and another word.

Name ____________________

"Ssssilly" Rabbit

Decide whether to add *-s* or *-es* to make each word plural.
Circle the letter in the correct column.

	add *-s*	add *-es*
1. box	O	R
2. rabbit	C	H
3. hat	A	S
4. glass	T	D
5. cape	O	A
6. fox	B	A
7. kiss	C	B
8. wand	R	H

Bonus Box: Write the plural words on the back of this page.

What does a magician say when he sees a snake?

To solve the riddle, write the circled letters from above on the numbered lines below.

"__ __ __ __ __ __ - __ __ __ __ __!"
6 7 1 3 4 3 2 5 7 8 6

Name ____

Rascal the Rabbit

Add *-s* or *-es* to the word below each line to make the word plural. Write the new word on the line.

1. Rascal causes lots of _____________ for Max.
   problem

2. He eats _____________ of carrots and lots of fruit.
   bunch

3. But sometimes he chews on other _____________.
   thing

4. Rascal chewed through the bands on two of Max's _____________.
   watch

5. And Max has to sew _____________ over the holes Rascal chews in his cape.
   patch

6. Rascal also likes to play _____________.
   trick

7. He hides under _____________ and behind benches.
   bush

8. Sometimes he even hides Max's magic _____________.
   hat

9. If Max had two _____________, the first one would be
   wish
   for Rascal to behave.

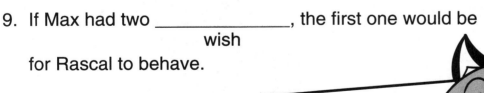

10. His second wish would be to find his magic _____________!
    wand

Name ______________________________

Pick a Card!

Write the plural form of each word.

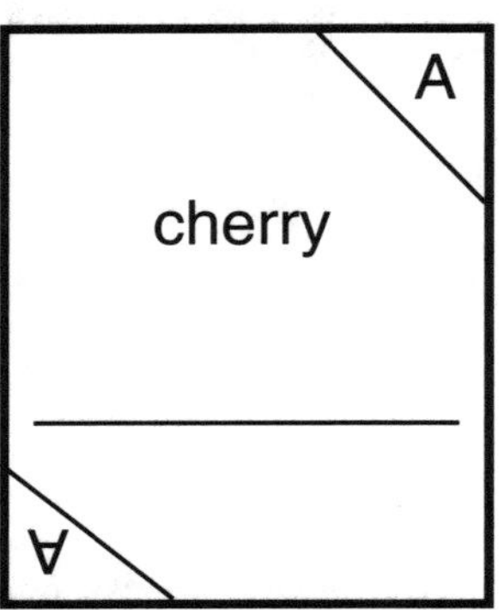
A
cherry
A

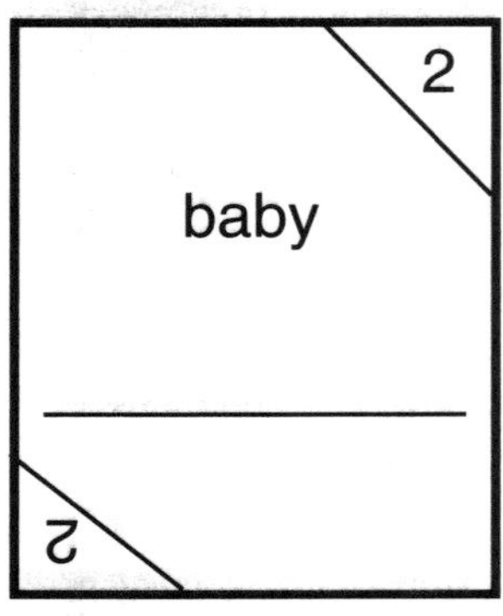
2
baby
2

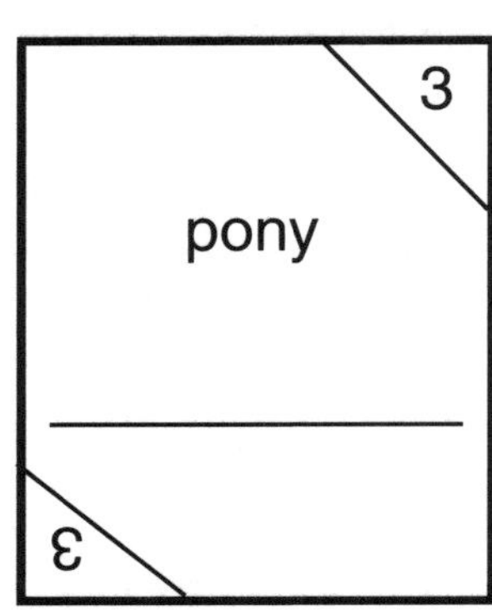
3
pony
3

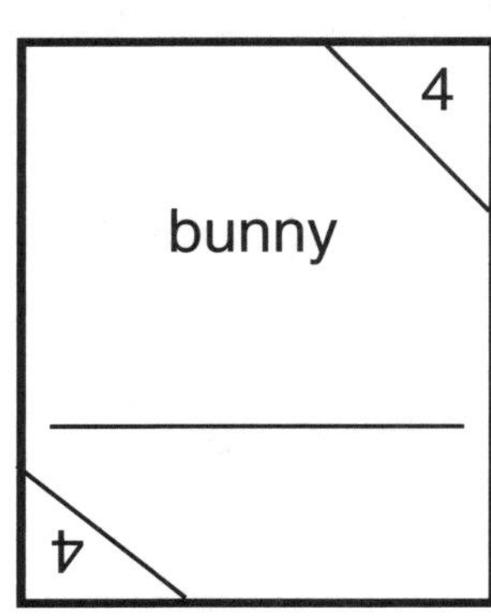
4
bunny
4

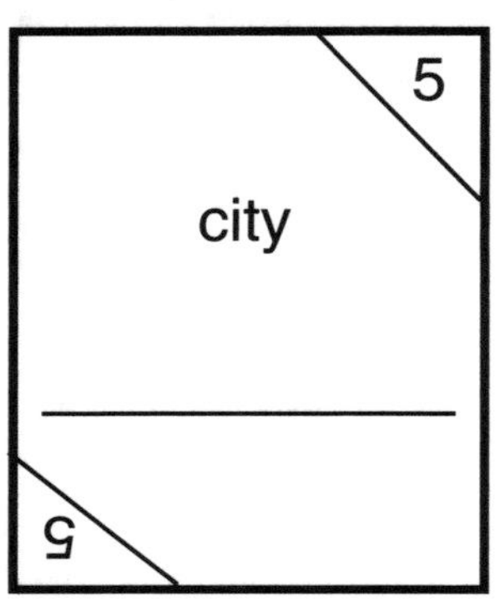
5
city
5

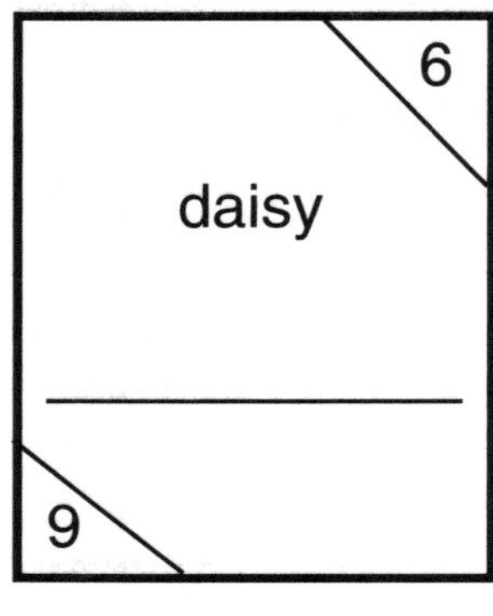
6
daisy
6

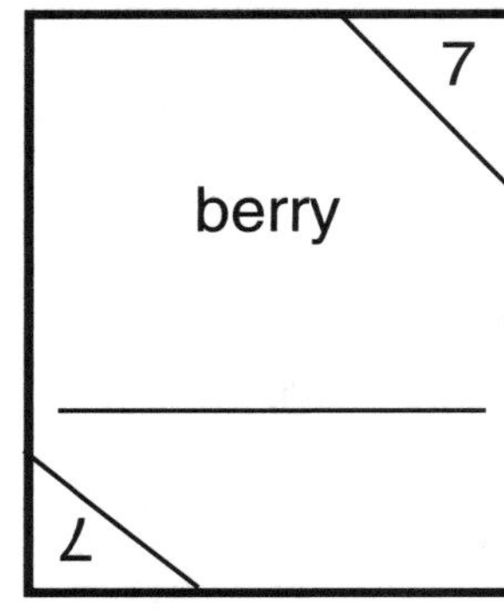
7
berry
7

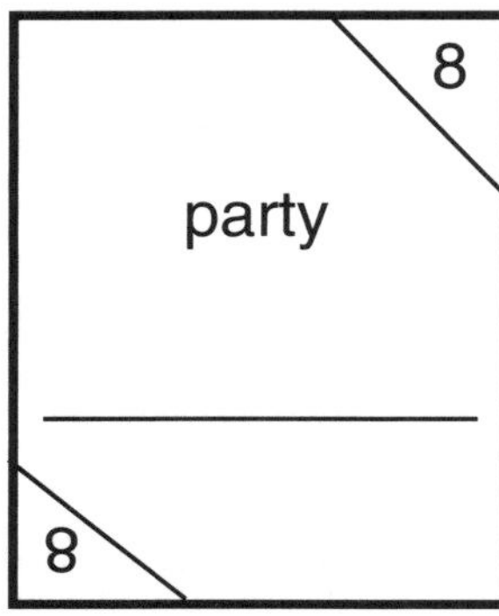
8
party
8

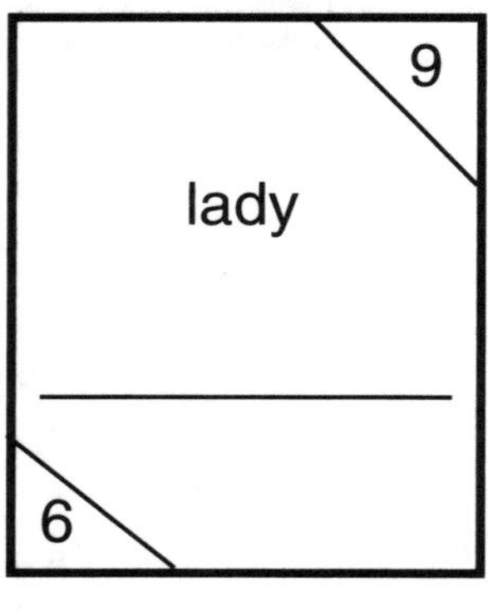
9
lady
9

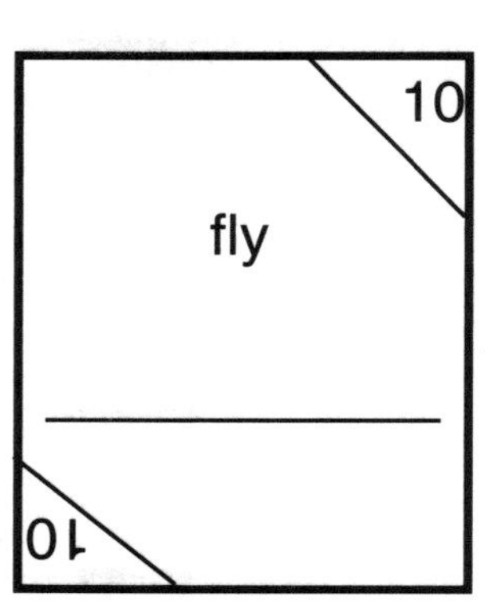
10
fly
10

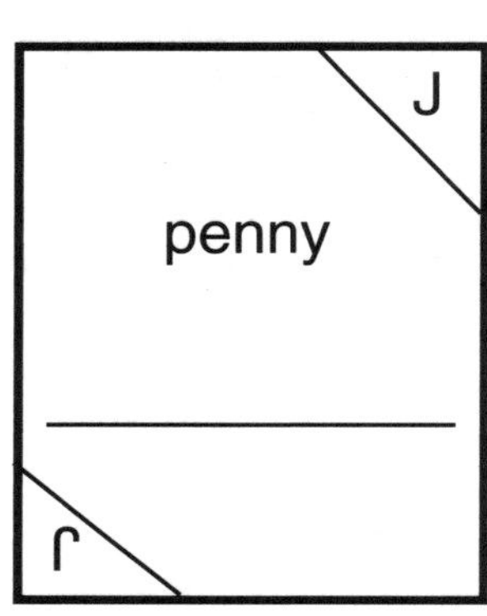
J
penny
J

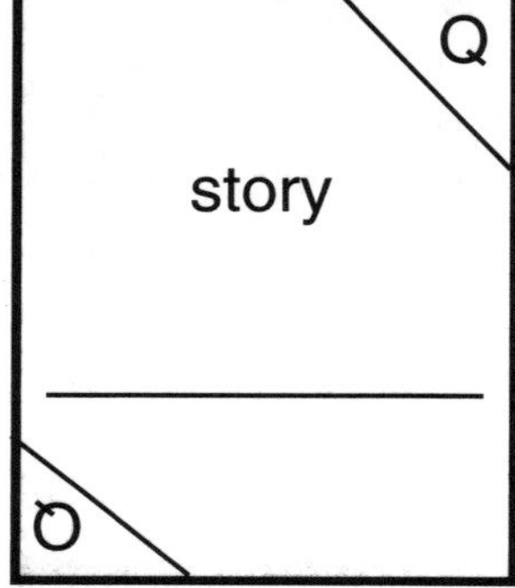
Q
story
Q

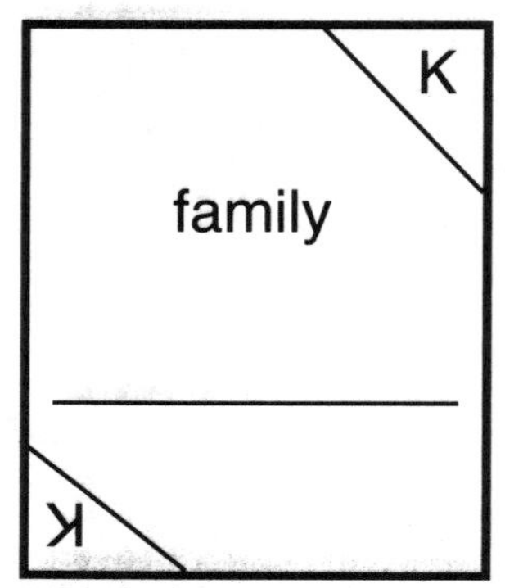
K
family
K

JOKER

Name ______________________________________

Rascal's Favorite Words

Write the plural form of each word.

1. goose ___ ___ ___ (___) ___	6. woman ___ (___) ___ ___ ___
2. ox ___ ___ ___ (___)	7. mouse ___ ___ ___ (___)
3. sheep ___ ___ ___ ___ (___)	8. foot ___ ___ ___ (___)
4. cactus ___ (___) ___ ___ ___	9. deer ___ (___) ___ ___
5. tooth ___ ___ ___ ___ (___)	10. child ___ ___ ___ (___) ___ ___ ___ ___

What are Rascal the Rabbit's favorite magic words?

To find out, unscramble the circled letters from above. Write them on the lines below.

___ ___ ___ ___ ___ ___ ___
and
___ ___ a ___ k
y ___ u

Name____

Shopping

Write *-s* or *-es* to make each word plural.
Cut out each word card.
Glue the card onto the matching shopping bag.

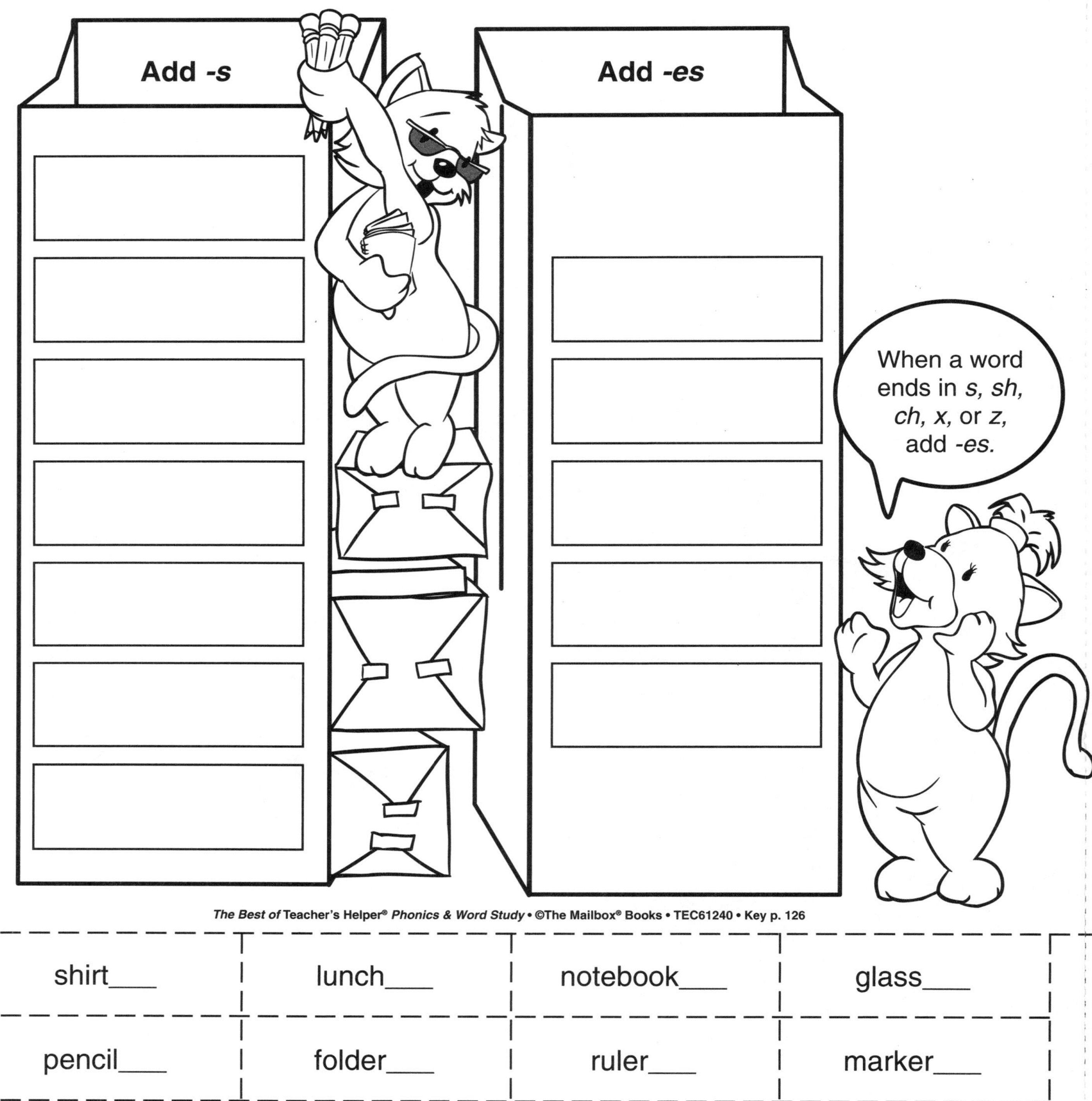
Add *-s*
Add *-es*
When a word ends in *s, sh, ch, x,* or *z,* add *-es.*

shirt___	lunch___	notebook___	glass___
pencil___	folder___	ruler___	marker___
toothbrush___	pencil box___	sock___	watch___

Name ______________________________

In the Rain

Write the plural for each word on the line.
Color each umbrella by the code.

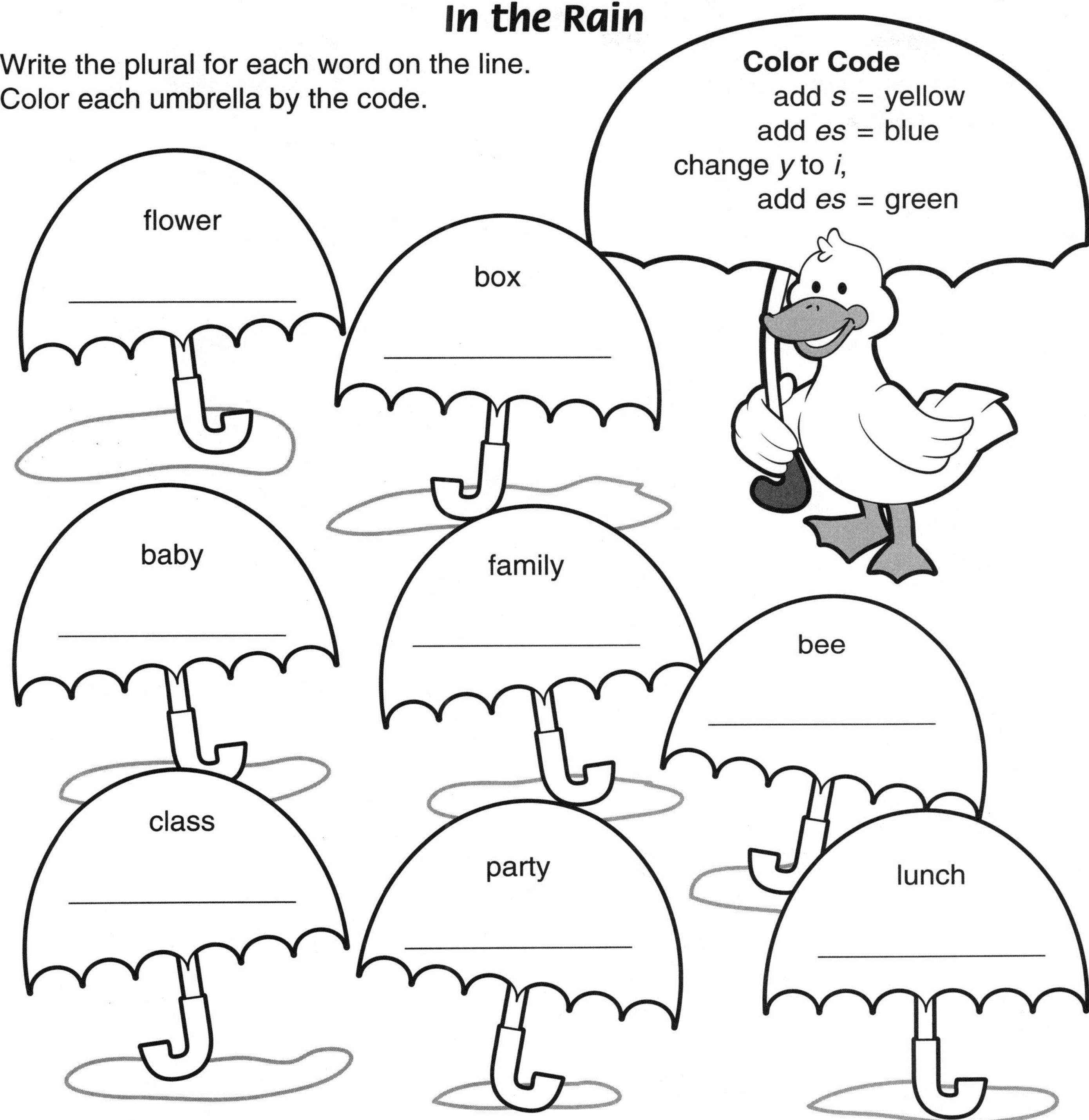
Color Code
add *s* = yellow
add *es* = blue
change *y* to *i*,
add *es* = green
flower
box
baby
family
bee
class
party
lunch

Complete each sentence by writing a different plural word from above.

1. People plant ______________ in the spring.
2. ______________ will buzz around the flowers.
3. ______________ will take trips to the park.

Name ________________________________

At the Bookstore

Add *-ed* to each base word.
Write the new word on the line.
Color by the code.

Color Code
Added *-ed* without changing the base word = orange
Dropped the final *e* before adding *-ed* = purple
Doubled the final consonant before adding *-ed* = green

love
____

skim

____

trip
____

taste
____

like
____

visit
____

pick
____

drop
____

open
____

shop
____

stack
____

share
____

Paula's Pages
Grand
Opening!

Bonus Box: On the back of this paper, write three sentences. Use at least one *-ed* word from above in each sentence.

Name ____________________

Bookstore Bookworms

Bookworms Welcome
at Paula's Pages!

Cut out the bookworms at the bottom of the page.
Glue a happy bookworm under each word that is spelled correctly.
Glue a sad bookworm under each word that is spelled incorrectly.
Write the misspelled words correctly.

1. solving ____________
2. browseing ____________
3. reading ____________
4. chating ____________
5. searching ____________
6. buying ____________
7. huming ____________
8. flying ____________
9. learnning ____________
10. runing ____________
11. picking ____________
12. jumpping ____________

Name ______________________________

Paula's Picks

Complete each title.
Add *-ed* or *-ing* to the base word under each line.
Write the new word on the line.

Learning
to Fly
by
U. R. Flying

1. A Day at the ____________ Cages
(Bat)
2. The Parrot That ____________ the World
(Save)
3. Parrots That ____________ Baseball
(Play)
4. Water Safety and ____________ Tips
(Bathe)
5. ____________ Bird, My Life as a Pet
(Cage)
6. ____________ the Zoo!
(Visit)
7. A Bird's Guide to ____________
(Soar)
8. How I ____________ to Fly
(Learn)
9. ____________ Down Good Food
(Track)
10. Coo! Coo! The Crowd ____________
(Cheer)
11. A Guide to Parrot ____________
(Race)
12. The Parrot That ____________ Its Perch
(Miss)

Bonus Box: Circle three words you added *-ing* to. On the back of this sheet, write each of these base words with *-ed* as an ending.

Name ____________________

Bird Words

Add *-ed* and *-ing* to each word.
Write the new words on the lines.
The first one has been done for you.

1. cluck
2. gobble
3. soar
4. perch
5. peck
6. hop
7. nest
8. swoop
9. glide
10. waddle
Welcome to Paula's Pages!
-ed
-ing
1. clucked
clucking
2.
3.
4.
5.
6.
7.
8.
9.
10.

Bonus Box: Six of the words on the books above do not change their spelling when you add *-ed* or *-ing.* Color the books with those words.

Name ____________________

Riding the Waves

Complete each sentence.
Add *-ed* to the base word in front of each sentence.
Write the new word on the line.
Color the sail by the code below.

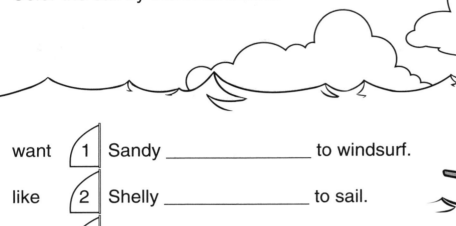

want	1	Sandy ______________ to windsurf.
like	2	Shelly ______________ to sail.
skim	3	They ______________ across the water.
switch	4	Then they ______________ with each other.
plan	5	They ______________ to try something new.
decide	6	Sandy ______________ they should snorkel.
laugh	7	They ______________ and played in the waves.
love	8	The friends ______________ their day at the ocean!

Color Code

added *-ed* without changing the base word = blue
dropped the final *e* before adding *-ed* = purple
doubled the final consonant before adding *-ed* = green

Bonus Box: Add *-ed* to the word *shop.* On the back of this page, write a sentence that includes the new word.

Name ____________________

Surfing Seals

Circle the word that best completes each sentence.
Be careful! Some words are not spelled correctly.

1. It's an ________ day for Sandy and Shelly.
   exciting exciteing excited

2. They're ________ surfing!
   gooing goed going

3. They start ________ to the water.
   runing runned running

4. Sandy starts ________.
   paddleing paddling paddled

5. Shelly begins ________ her feet.
   kicking kickking kicked

6. The friends are ________ through the water.
   racing raccing raceing

7. They sit ________ for a big wave.
   waitting waited waiting

8. Then they see it ________ !
   comming coming comeing

9. ________ up, they catch the wave!
   Jumpping Jumping Jump

10. They are a pair of ________ seals!
    surfing surffing surfeing

Name ____________________

Snorkeling Seals

Write each new word on the lines.
Follow the spelling rules.

Spelling Rules

1. If a word ends with a short vowel and one consonant, double the consonant. Then add *-ed* or *-ing.*
2. If a word ends with e, drop the *e.* Then add *-ed* or *-ing.*
3. If a word ends with *y,* change the *y* to *i.* Then add *-ed.*

1. cry + ed = ____________
2. jog + ed = ____________
3. carry + ed = ____________
4. dive + ing = ____________
5. talk + ed = ____________
6. swim + ing = ____________
7. smile + ed = ____________
8. hop + ed = ____________
9. surf + ing = ____________
10. want + ed = ____________
11. take + ing = ____________
12. move + ing = ____________
13. wash + ed = ____________
14. laugh + ing = ____________
15. try + ed = ____________
16. run + ing = ____________
17. wave + ed = ____________
18. plan + ing = ____________
19. hurry + ed = ____________
20. give + ing = ____________

Name ______________________________ Inflectional Endings

-s, -ed, -ing

Spitting Seeds

Cut apart the word-ending cards below.
Glue each one on a box to complete a word.

1.  June enjoy 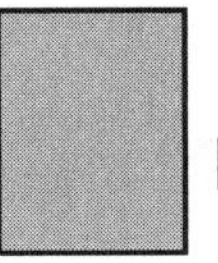 picnics!
2. This morning, she ask  Wally whether he wanted to go.
3. Wally couldn't wait to get start 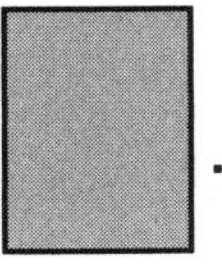 .
4. June began pack 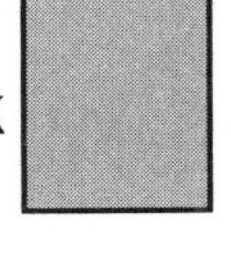 a basket full of food.
5. Wally love  to eat fruit.
6. The friends started look  for a perfect spot.
7. June like  to sit under the trees.
8. The friends sat and began eat  their fruit.
9. Wally always count  the seeds in his piece.
10. When it started to get dark, June and Wally head  home.

s	s	s	s	ed	ed	ed	ing	ing	ing

Name ____

The Pool Is Open!

Use the code to fill in each △ and □.
Choose a root word from the word bank to complete each sentence.

Prefix Code
re
un

1. The water in the indoor pool was dark and □ ___ ___ ____________.
2. It was □ ___ ___ ____________ to swim in the pool, so the staff went to work.
3. First, they had to □ ___ ___ ____________ the drain.
4. Next, they had to △ ___ ___ ____________ the lane lines.
5. Then the ladder was △ ___ ___ ____________.
6. Finally, the pool was cleaned and △ ___ ___ ____________.
7. Now, many families want to △ ___ ___ ____________ their memberships.
8. Some kids who have been gone for a while have △ ___ ___ ____________.
9. It is an □ ___ ___ ____________ group of swimmers.
10. But it is no longer □ ___ ___ ____________ to be seen at the pool!

Word Bank
paint
clog
clean
filled
appeared
new
cool
safe
usual
placed

Name ____________________

Making a Splash!

Look at the words below.
Write the letter for the word that matches each definition.

1. opposite of appear ______
2. before a sale ______
3. heat before ______
4. opposite of respect ______
5. before a game ______
6. opposite of agree ______
7. before a drill ______
8. opposite of obey ______
9. opposite of like ______
10. pay before ______
11. test before ______
12. opposite of believe ______

A
prepay
B
disappear
C
dislike
D
pregame
E
disbelieve
F
preheat
G
presale
H
predrill
I
disobey
J
disagree
K
pretest
L
disrespect

Name ______________________

Adult Swim!

Add each word in the word bank to one of the prefixes.
Write each new word in the matching pool lane.

Word Bank				
marine	read	spell	way	place
zero	judge	copy	floor	soil

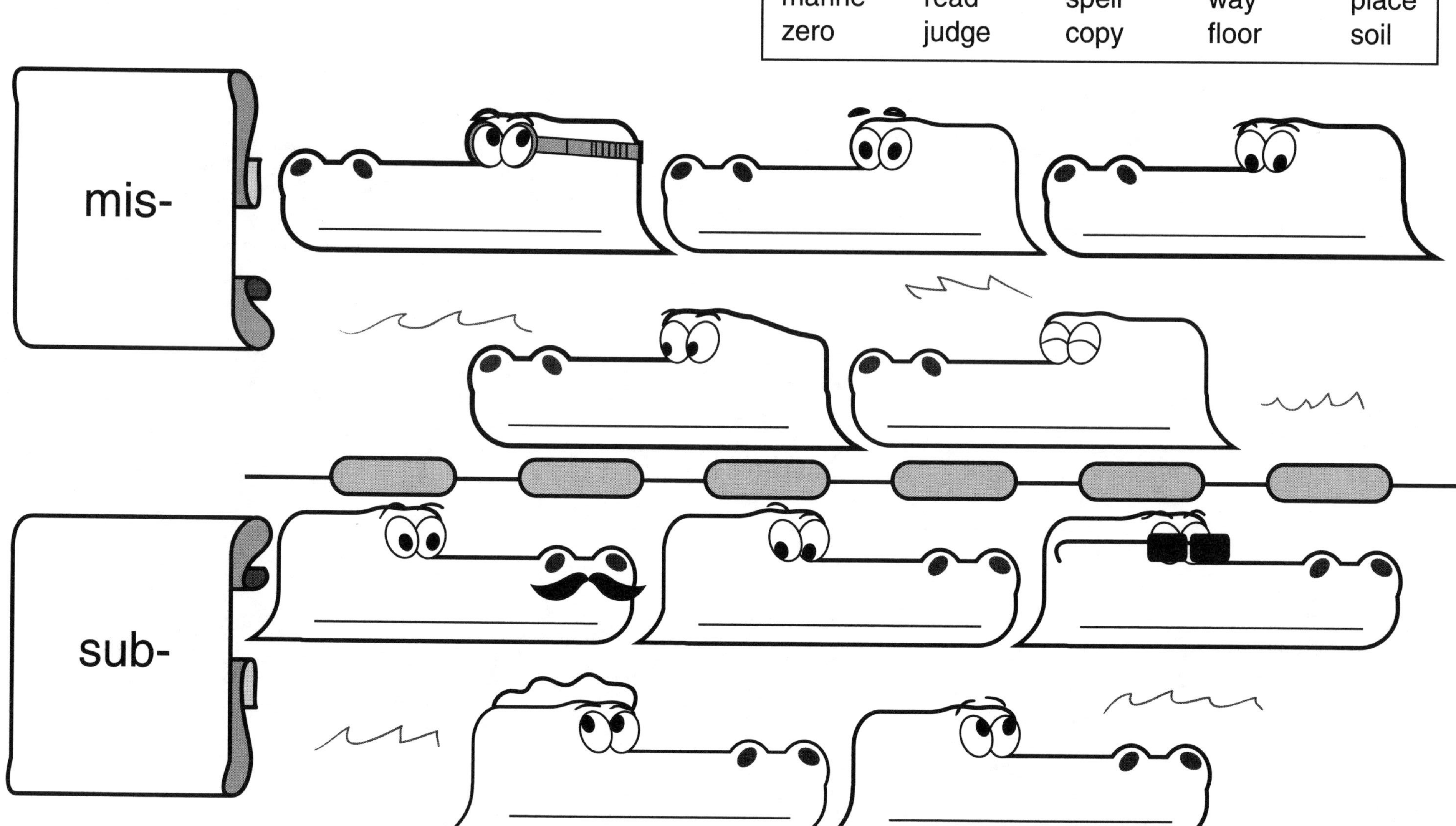
mis-
sub-

Name ____________________

"Sew" Much Information!

Add *-er* or *-est* to each root word to make a word that completes the sentence. Write the new word on the line.

Add *-er* when you compare two items. Add *-est* when you compare three or more items.

1. This blue ribbon is ____________ (wide) than the red ribbon.
2. Knitting needles are ____________ (dull) than sewing needles.
3. The velvet is the ____________ (soft) fabric of all.
4. Floss is ____________ (thin) than yarn.
5. These pillows are the ____________ (thick) in the store.
6. Flora is the ____________ (fast) seamstress working here.
7. Purple fabric is ____________ (dark) than gray fabric.
8. Cotton thread is the ____________ (strong) thread we sell.
9. These scissors are the ____________ (sharp) in the store.
10. Silver buttons are ____________ (cheap) than gold buttons.

Name ____________________

A Flamingo With Flair

Read the definition below each line.
Add *-ful* or *-less* to a word from the word bank to make a new word that matches the definition.
Write the new word on the line.

1. Every day, Flora's ______________ customers come to the fabric store.
   (full of faith)

2. Without Flora, they are ______________.
   (without help)

3. The customers are ______________ to know Flora.
   (full of thanks)

4. Her sewing is ______________.
   (without flaws)

5. She makes the work look ______________.
   (without effort)

6. She is always kind and ______________.
   (full of thought)

7. People love the ______________ fabric she uses.
   (full of color)

8. Everyone agrees that Flora's work is ______________.
   (without price)

Word Bank

effort, color, price, help, faith, flaw, thought, thank

Bonus Box: On the back of this page, write two sentences. Use at least one of the new words from above in each sentence.

Name______________________________

Strings and Things

Look at each word in the word bank.
Add *-able* or *-ness* to each word.
Write each new word on a spool in the correct stack.

-ness
-able

Word Bank

bend	remark
do	dark
kind	refill
fix	sad
soft	paint
sick	slow
wash	great
break	weak
fair	wear

Name ______________________________

What a Racket!

Write *-able* or *-ful* to make new words.
Circle the words in the puzzle.

1. pass________
2. pride________
3. fix________
4. thank________
5. use________
6. stretch________
7. hope________
8. power________
9. wash________
10. truth________

u	l	v	d	g	y	b	i	f	r	o	h	p	r	i	d	e	f	u	l	f	x	o
s	t	r	e	t	c	h	a	b	l	e	o	c	i	v	o	g	h	p	k	i	r	v
e	d	c	l	b	z	a	h	i	s	q	p	w	a	s	h	a	b	l	e	x	l	n
f	z	s	b	r	c	a	y	u	g	r	e	p	m	h	u	l	p	i	w	a	y	h
u	m	p	o	w	e	r	f	u	l	j	f	n	j	b	p	a	s	s	a	b	l	e
l	e	m	k	t	d	t	f	x	u	p	u	k	t	r	u	t	h	f	u	l	j	a
e	t	f	n	t	h	a	n	k	f	u	l	f	w	a	d	k	q	e	q	e	m	w

Name ____

Mixed-Up Mittens

Look at the underlined part on each mitten.
Color the mitten if the underlined word is the base word.

rewind
preschool
untie
disappear
reread
subway
mislead
preview
disagree
uncover
submarine
misuse
rerun
unhappy

Name ______________________

Some Snow to Throw!

Write the base word below each word.

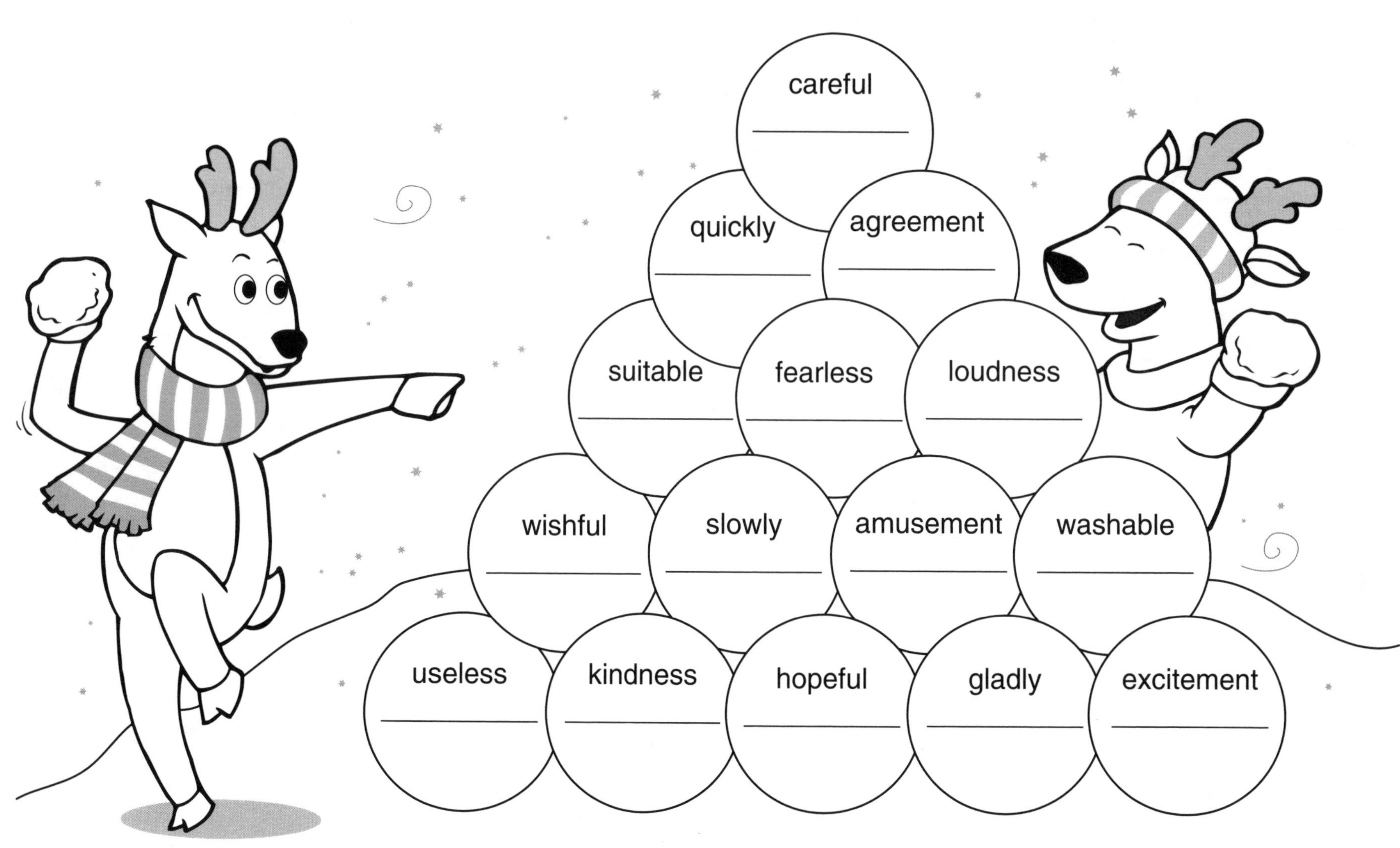
careful
quickly
agreement
suitable
fearless
loudness
wishful
slowly
amusement
washable
useless
kindness
hopeful
gladly
excitement

Name ____________________

Reindeer Games

Circle the base word in each word in the word bank.
Complete each sentence with a different base word.

Word Bank

joyful	replay
preheat	quickly
enjoyable	sleepless
retry	wishful
coldness	lovely
endless	rebuild

1. The reindeer like to ______________ in the snow.
2. They ______________ sledding down the hill.
3. They may have a ______________ snowball fight.
4. They run and ______________ to hide from each other.
5. Everyone is snowy by the ______________.
6. The friends also ______________ to make snow forts.
7. They ______________ the walls so high!
8. It's fun to play when it's really ______________ outside!
9. Playing all day brings everyone ______________.
10. The deer ______________ they could play all night.
11. At home, they ______________ up some cocoa.
12. Then everyone is ready to go to ______________.

Bonus Box: On the back of this page, write two words that each start with the prefix *un*. Then write two words that each end with the suffix *ly*.

Name ______________________________

A Spelling Slide

Look at the words on the slide.
In each pair of words, circle the word that is spelled correctly.

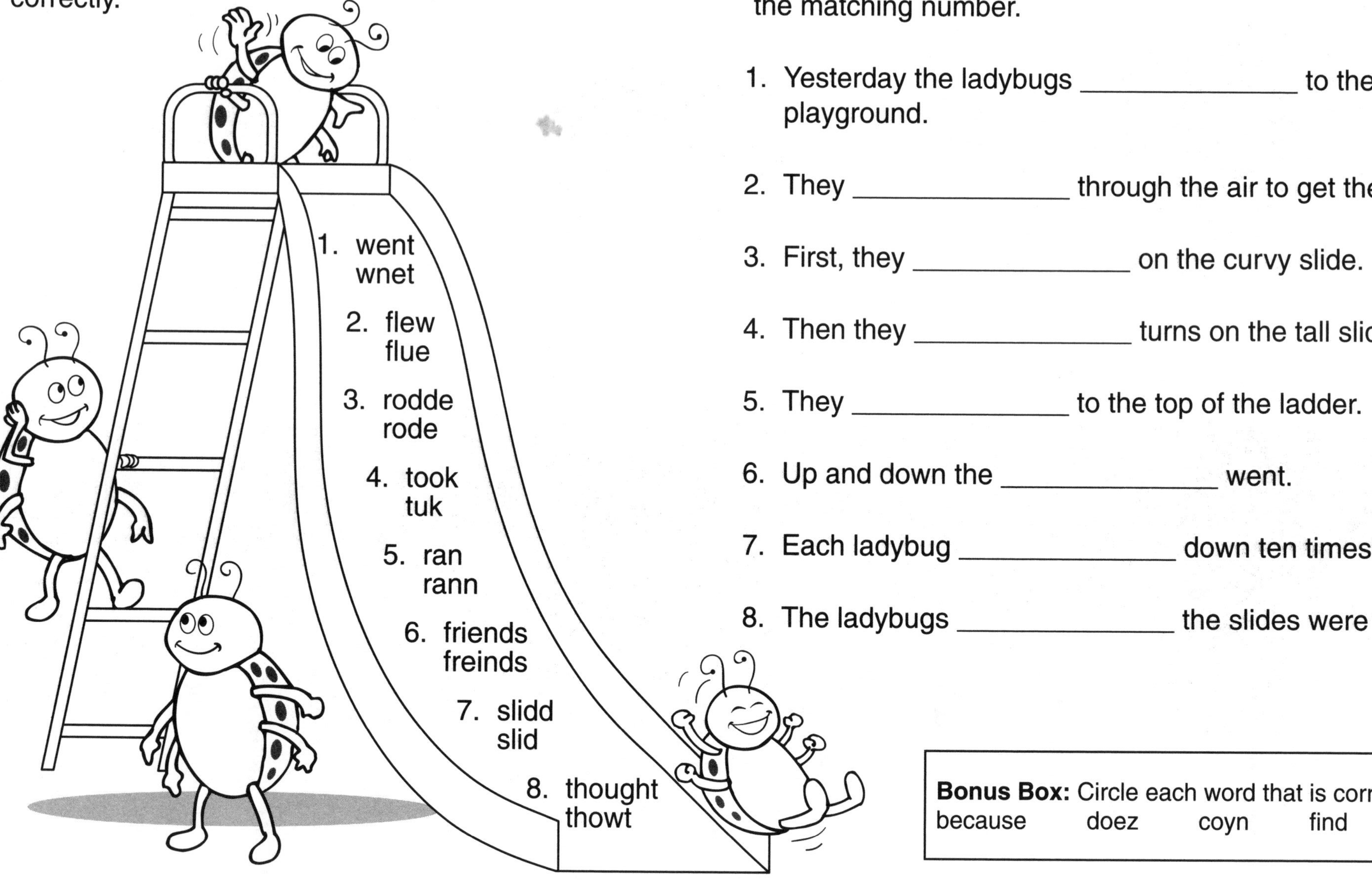
1. went
wnet
2. flew
flue
3. rodde
rode
4. took
tuk
5. ran
rann
6. friends
freinds
7. slidd
slid
8. thought
thowt

Complete each sentence by writing the circled word from the matching number.

1. Yesterday the ladybugs ______________ to the playground.
2. They ______________ through the air to get there.
3. First, they ______________ on the curvy slide.
4. Then they ______________ turns on the tall slide.
5. They ______________ to the top of the ladder.
6. Up and down the ______________ went.
7. Each ladybug ______________ down ten times!
8. The ladybugs ______________ the slides were fun!

Bonus Box: Circle each word that is correct.
because doez coyn find

Name ____________________

Swinging and Singing

Draw a line through each word that is not spelled correctly.
Write the word correctly above the misspelled word.
For each word you correct, color a ladybug's spot.

Three ladybug freinds met at the park. They stood on the playgrownd and looked around. There where so many things to do! Thay chose to go on the swings furst. Each ladybug sat on a swing and swung hi in the air. It felt grate to go so high! They talked and sang together. Then they rode thee merry-go-round. They spun around untill they were dizzy. Wat a fun day for the three spotted friends!

Name ____________________

Ups and Downs

Cut apart the ladybug cards below.
Set aside the cards that have words that are spelled incorrectly.
Glue each correct word card on a box on the seesaw.

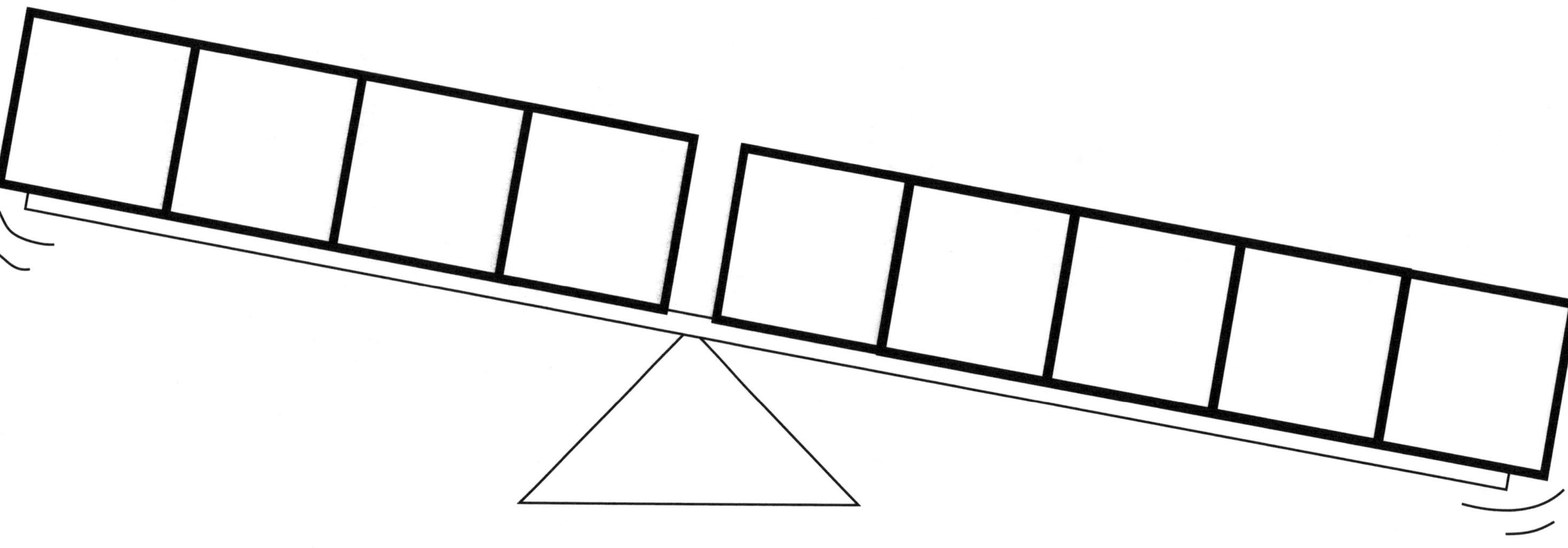

farr	spaek	bought	bilt	leave	sold	buye	spoke	keppt
doez	told	welkum	drew	shook	left	pensil	nevr	not

Page 4

1. cat	8. X
2. dip	9. X
3. X	10. X
4. cap	11. sip
5. van	12. sad
6. pig	13. man
7. X	14. X

Page 5

1. wet	7. log
2. web	8. hog
3. wed	9. dog
4. bed	10. dot
5. beg	11. cot
6. leg	12. cob

Bonus Box: The word *dot* should be written along with five words that rhyme with it, such as *not, pot, hot, lot,* and *got*.

Page 6

1. has	6. rags
2. but	7. fun
3. mugs, cups, pans	8. pat
4. tub	9. hug
5. suds	10. dad

Bonus Box: Answers will vary.

Page 7

1. tub	8. top
2. bag	9. pin
3. gem	10. nut
4. men	11. tag
5. nap	12. gum
6. pop	13. map
7. pit	14. pet

Page 8

1. Sunday	5. last
2. cat	6. fun
3. passing	7. can
4. runs	8. just

Bonus Box: Answers will vary.

Page 9

1. yell	6. Then
2. best	7. block
3. job	8. well
4. clock	9. tell
5. referee	10. top

Page 10

1. kick	6. trip
2. miss	7. hit
3. wish	8. quit
4. win	9. switch
5. rip	10. fix

Page 11

It was a close, exciting game, but the Wildcats beat the Tigers by seven points. The two teams were running up and down the field all through the game. Each kicker kicked a field goal. The receivers made many catches. The quarterbacks threw perfect passes. The players who block were blocking every play! The crowd stood up and clapped. The referees blew their whistles. Everyone thought it was a great game! And even though the Tigers lost, they had lots of fun playing!

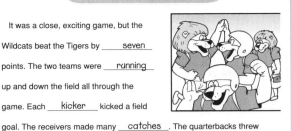

bl o cking
c a tches
cl a pped
k i cker
r e ferees
r u nning
wh i stles
s e ven
l o ts
u p

Page 12

1. stone	2. toad	3. soap	4. home
5. road	6. rope	7. bone	8. close
9. coat	10. boat	11. goal	12. stove

Page 13

1. Put butter and eggs into a large bowl.
2. Blend the mixture on low speed.
3. Slowly add flour and sugar.
4. Put the whole mix into the refrigerator.
5. Close the lid.
6. Wait until the mixture is cold.
7. Then roll it out flat.
8. Use cookie cutters to make roses and other shapes.
9. Place the cookies in rows on trays.
10. Go ask an adult to help you with the baking.

Bonus Box: Answers will vary. Possible answers include *bold, fold, gold, hold,* and *old.*

Page 14

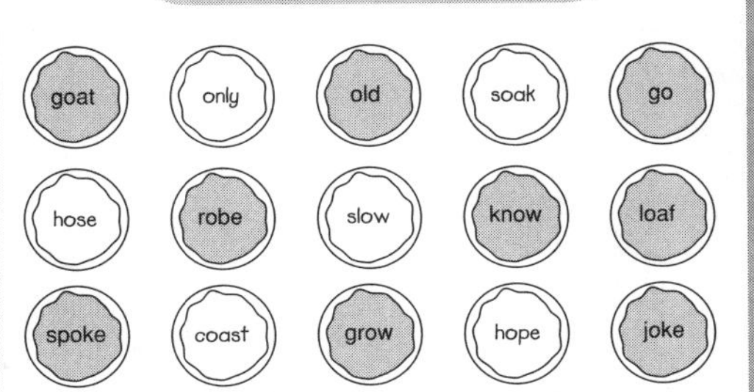

goat
only
old
soak
go
hose
robe
slow
know
loaf
spoke
coast
grow
hope
joke

Page 15

~~Crains~~ on the ~~Lak~~
Cranes Lake

~~Paenting~~ the ~~Gait~~
Painting Gate

A ~~Vas~~ in the ~~Baen~~
Vase Rain

~~Caik~~ on a ~~Plat~~
Cake Plate

A ~~Waeter~~ on ~~Skats~~
Waiter Skates

~~Plains~~ and ~~Treans~~
Planes Trains

Bonus Box: Answers will vary.

Page 16

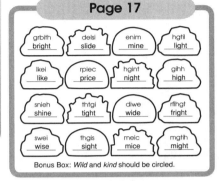

wheat, tree, year, seat, deep, teeth, meal, east, need, bee, heap, feel

```
  o v j m e a l
q b e e w h l x d
k n t m h e y u e
g e b j e t r e e
y e a r a a h c p
h d l e t p e e h
e r z f g i a a p
  t e e t h p s
  c s e a t f t
  b w l o q a e
```

Page 17

grbith / bright	delsi / slide	enim / mine	hgtil / light
lkei / like	rpiec / price	hgint / night	gihh / high
snieh / shine	thtgi / tight	diwe / wide	rflhgt / fright
swei / wise	thgis / sight	meic / mice	mgtih / might

Bonus Box: *Wild* and *kind* should be circled.

Page 18

1. There are many things to sea at the museum.
2. I liek to look at the rocks.
3. Carl likes to see the paentings.
4. Chloe loves to be in the room with the vaises.
5. Eeach of us likes to see the dinosaur models.
6. I like to visit the museum every yeer.
7. Next tiem, I want to see the mummies!
8. I would like to see the cav exhibit too.
9. My brother nedes to go with me.
10. He likes the syte of mummies too!
11. I will ask Mom to taek us.
12. She mite like to visit the museum with us.

Order may vary.

see	time
like	cave
paintings	needs
vases	sight
Each	take
year	might

Page 19

1. toast	2. smoke	3. show	4. coat
5. burrow	6. slow	7. toad	8. rope
9. boat	10. stone	11. bone	12. pillow

He likes "chicken" out his books!

Page 20

Ray Rooster loves to read. His class visits the library each week. This time, Ray is looking for a cookbook. He wants to cook a meal using wheat and seeds. Ray looks without making a peep. The book is not easy to find. The librarian, Ms. Sweet, will help him succeed. She knows that they need to check the computer. Together, they'll use it to find what they're seeking. The librarian wheels over a ladder and reaches up to the top shelf. "Thanks!" says Ray. "Our search is complete!"

j w h e a t b q a
w f e s r p e e p
h n r e a c h e s
e s e e k i n g y
e u a d n l p m c
l c d s w e e t k
s c o m p l e t e
h e r e o d a d a
w e t a g z c m s
h d a l u s h x y

Page 21

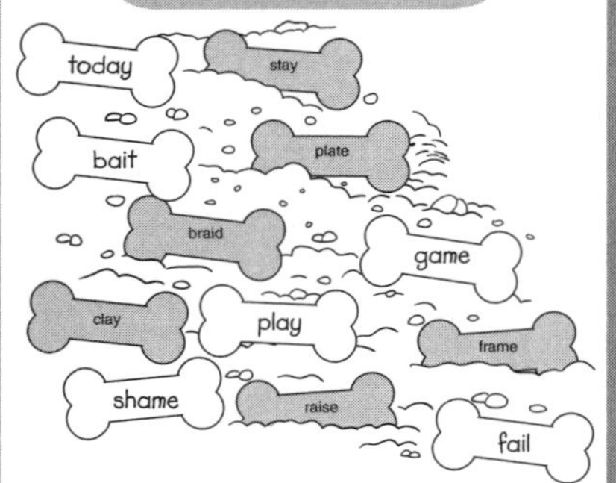

today
stay
bait
plate
braid
game
clay
play
frame
shame
raise
fail

Page 22

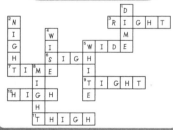

1 DIME (down)
2 NIGHT (down)
3 RIGHT (across)
4 WISE (down)
5 WIDE (across)
5 WHITE (down)
6 SIGH (across)
7 TIME (across)
8 MIGHT (down)
9 TIGHT (across)
10 HIGH (across)
11 THIGH (across)

Page 23

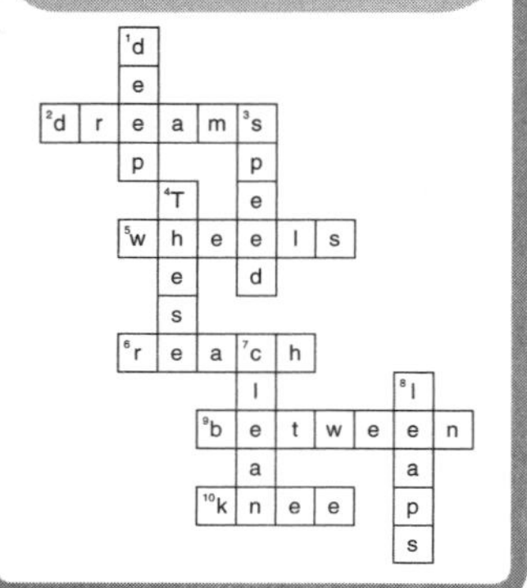

Page 24

1.	rope	7.	soap
2.	coat	8.	stove
3.	smoke	9.	coach
4.	toad	10.	joke
5.	stone	11.	broken
6.	goal	12.	road

Page 25

Order may vary.

long *e*	**long *o***
teach	home
agreed	float
treat	hole
seems	road
street	nose
meet	groans
see	coasts
	those

Page 26

1. grain	2. thankful	3. dash	4. blank
5. flashes	6. pain	7. strain	8. tank
9. prank	10. strained	11. rashes	12. raindrop
13. chain	14. cash	15. bashful	16. lanky
17. eyelash	18. Frank	19. brains	20. ashes

Bonus Box: Answers will vary.

Page 27

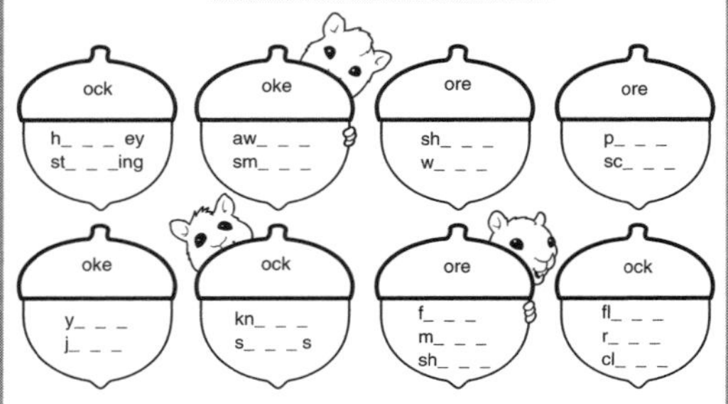

ock
h___ey
st___ing
oke
aw___
sm___
ore
sh___
w___
ore
p___
sc___
oke
y___
j___
ock
kn___
s___s
ore
f___
m___
sh___
ock
fl___
r___
cl___

Bonus Box: Mark wants to take more pictures of the seashore, but his camera is broken.

Page 28

1.	Lake	7.	came
2.	makes	8.	plates
3.	name	9.	bake
4.	fame	10.	late
5.	same	11.	sake
6.	cakes	12.	take

Page 29

Order may vary.

-in	sp_ _ach	v_ _egar	pumpk_ _ pie	rolling p_ _
-ip	bacon str_ _s	chip cl_ _s	onion d_ _	potato ch_ _s
-it	spl_ _ peas	taco k_ _	peach p_ _s	bacon b_ _s

Page 30

1. right	2. nine	3. tight
4. bride	5. mine	6. knight
7. pride	8. shine	9. wide
10. hide	11. pine	12. night

Page 31

Answers may vary. Possible answers include

-ock		-op		-ot	
sock	flock	hop	flop	got	hot
knock	clock	drop	chop	knot	pot
shock	rock	pop	clop	clot	shot
		shop		rot	

Page 32

***-ill* Clues**
1. fill
2. chill
3. still
4. pill
5. will

***-ink* Clues**
1. think
2. pink
3. wink
4. drink

***-ip* Clues**
1. chip
2. drip
3. flip
4. ship
5. snip
6. trip

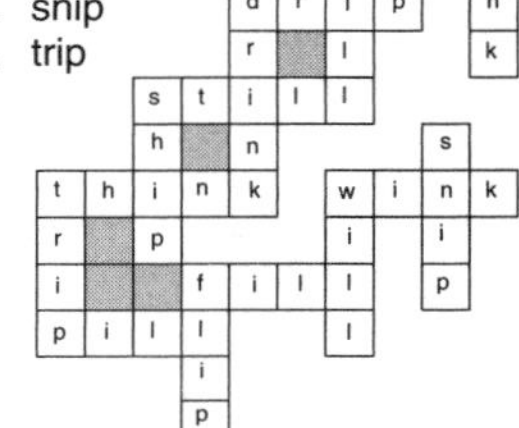

Page 33

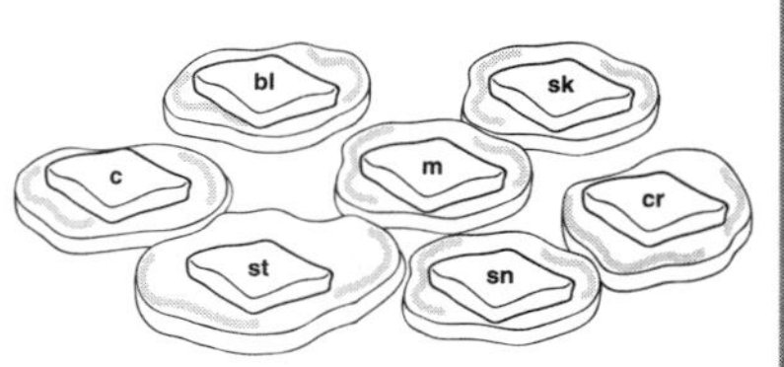

bl
sk
c
m
cr
st
sn

Bonus Box: Answers will vary. Possible answers include back, pack, sack, shack, and tack.

Page 34

1. rest	9. sell
2. fell	10. west
3. seat	11. smell
4. bell	12. neat
5. treat	13. nest
6. yell	14. test
7. best	15. meat
8. heat	

Page 35

1. b r an, **O**
2. b l ack, **Y**
3. b r ead, **O**
4. b l ue, **Y**
5. b l ast, **Y**
6. b r ide, **O**
7. b r ick, **O**
8. b l end, **Y**
9. b r other, **O**
10. b l ock, **Y**
11. b l aze, **Y**
12. b r oad, **O**
13. b l uff, **Y**
14. b l ess, **Y**
15. b l ind, **Y**
16. b r ace, **O**

Page 36

1. climb
2. crayon
3. cream
4. cling
5. close
6. clay
7. crumb
8. clip
9. craft
10. cricket
11. click
12. cross
13. clean
14. crab

Bonus Box: Answers will vary.

Page 37

1. frost
2. friends
3. from
4. floor
5. flap
6. flop
7. free
8. fluffy
9. flashy
10. flat
11. frowns
12. freeze

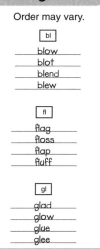

a	j	f	d	n	f	g	i	s
m	f	l	o	o	r	f	f	a
f	r	o	m	f	o	r	l	t
e	i	p	b	l	w	o	a	f
f	e	h	o	a	n	s	s	l
r	n	c	k	t	s	t	h	a
e	d	f	l	u	f	f	y	p
e	s	f	r	e	e	z	e	b

Bonus Box: Answers will vary.

Page 38

	-ank	-ing	-ock	-own	-ush
br-		bring		brown	brush
cl-	clank	cling	clock	clown	
cr-	crank		crock	crown	crush
fl-	flank	fling	flock	flown	flush
fr-	frank		frock	frown	

Page 39

s p in
s w im
s p ark
s c arf
s w eet
s p ace
s w ing
s p eed
s c old
s w itch
s w eep
s p eak
s c ary
s c ale

Page 40

Order may vary.

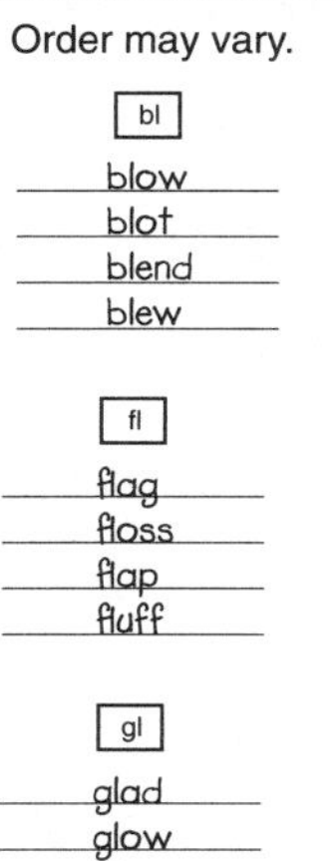

bl
blow
blot
blend
blew
fl
flag
floss
flap
fluff
gl
glad
glow
glue
glee

Page 41

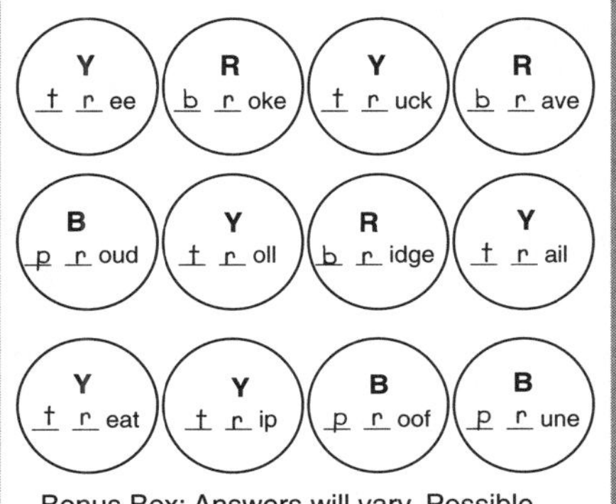

Y t r ee
R b r oke
Y t r uck
R b r ave
B p r oud
Y t r oll
R b r idge
Y t r ail
Y t r eat
Y t r ip
B p r oof
B p r une

Bonus Box: Answers will vary. Possible answers include *grow, grab, grin, grit, grid, grease,* and *growl.*

Page 42

1. clear
2. cloud
3. crab
4. creek
5. crate
6. cloth
7. clean
8. crow
9. crisp
10. craft
11. club
12. cry

Bonus Box: Answers will vary. Possible answers include *crowd, cream, crown, crack, crawl,* and *cricket.*

Page 43

HATS FOR HEADS
Our hats are the be s t, from ea s t to we s t.
Hurry, hurry while they la s t! With these low prices, they're going fa s t!
Don't dri f t by, stop in!
Please use the door on the le f t.
A hat makes a great gi f t!
Beat the heat! Protect your sca l p!
He l p wanted: part-time sales
All hats are made of the fine s t so f t fabrics.

Page 44

1. wasp
2. kept
3. golf
4. crisp
5. crept
6. gasp
7. shelf
8. wolf
9. swept
10. elf
11. slept
12. grasp

Bonus Box:
1. brown
2. green
3. blue
4. brown
5. green
6. brown
7. blue
8. blue
9. green
10. blue
11. green
12. brown

Page 45

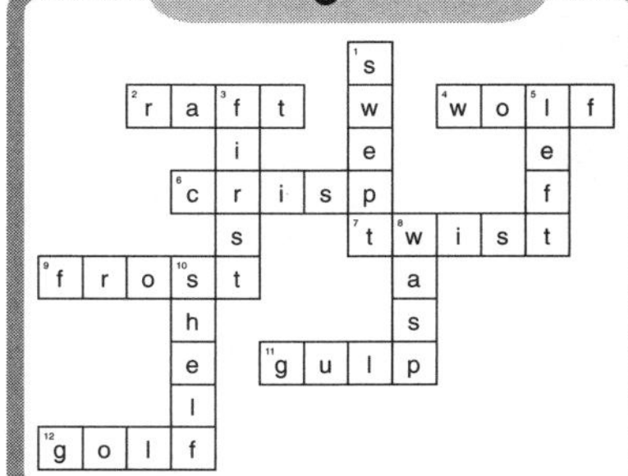

craft
wolf
crisp
twist
frost
gulp
golf
swept
first
left
wasp
shelf

Page 46

whistle
wrong
while
written
whale
wrote
wrinkle
wriggle
why
wheat
wrench
where
wrap
whopper

Bonus Box: Answers will vary but should include two of the following words: *when, why, who,* and *what.*

Page 47

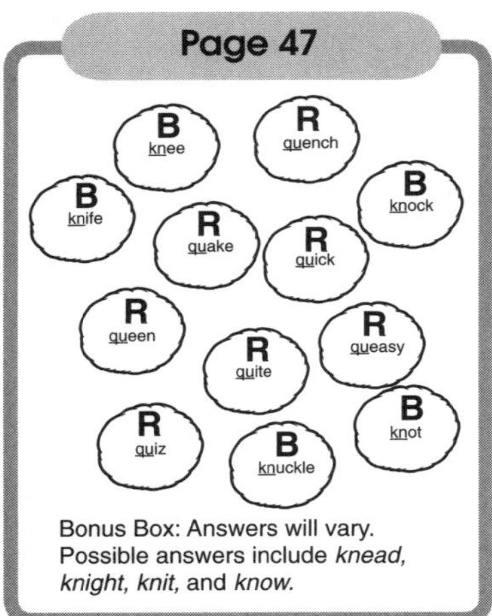

B knee
R quench
B knife
B knock
R quake
R quick
R queen
R quite
R queasy
R quiz
B knuckle
B knot

Bonus Box: Answers will vary. Possible answers include *knead, knight, knit,* and *know.*

Page 52

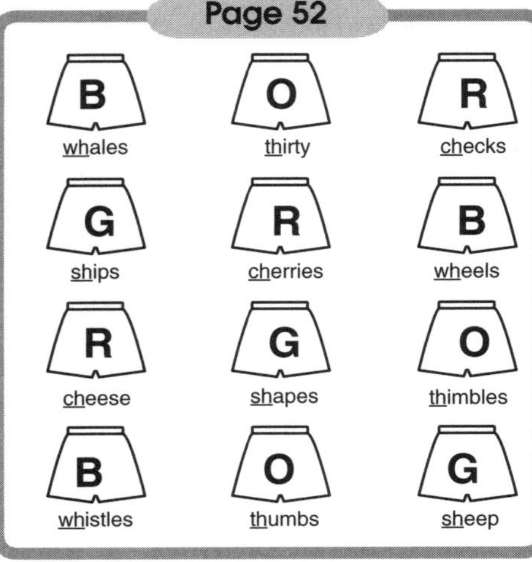

B whales
O thirty
R checks
G ships
R cherries
B wheels
R cheese
G shapes
O thimbles
B whistles
O thumbs
G sheep

Page 56

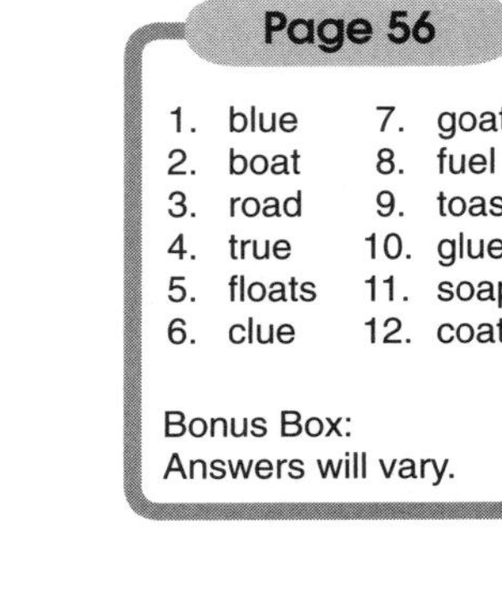

1.	blue	7.	goat
2.	boat	8.	fuel
3.	road	9.	toast
4.	true	10.	glue
5.	floats	11.	soap
6.	clue	12.	coat

Bonus Box:
Answers will vary.

Page 48

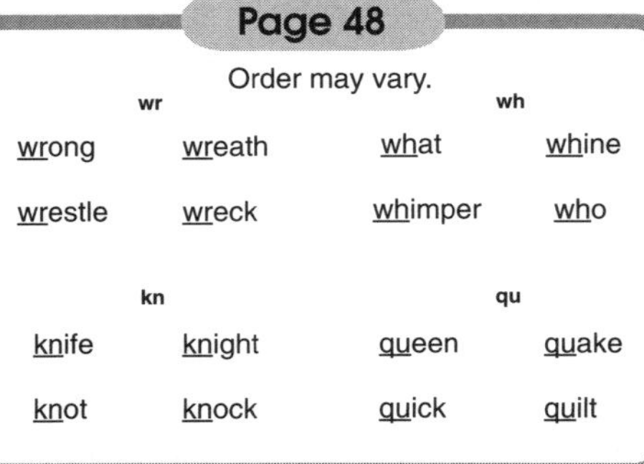
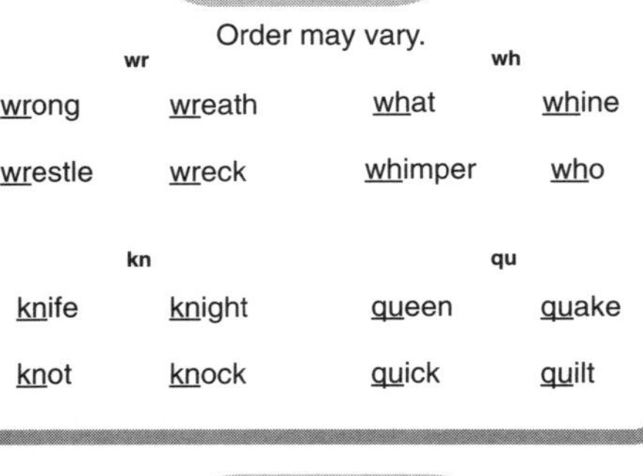

Order may vary.

wr		wh	
wrong	wreath	what	whine
wrestle	wreck	whimper	who

kn		qu	
knife	knight	queen	quake
knot	knock	quick	quilt

Page 53

1. month
2. with
3. health
4. such
5. beach
6. both
7. rush
8. splash
9. fish
10. much
11. truth
12. stylish

Page 57

G maid
R soap
B blue
Y mayor
R float
Y today
Y pay
G sail
Y spray
R road
G nail
B untrue
B glue
R coat
Y bay
G paint
Y trays
G daisy
Y maybe
B cruel
Y gray
R toast
Y replay
G plain

Page 49

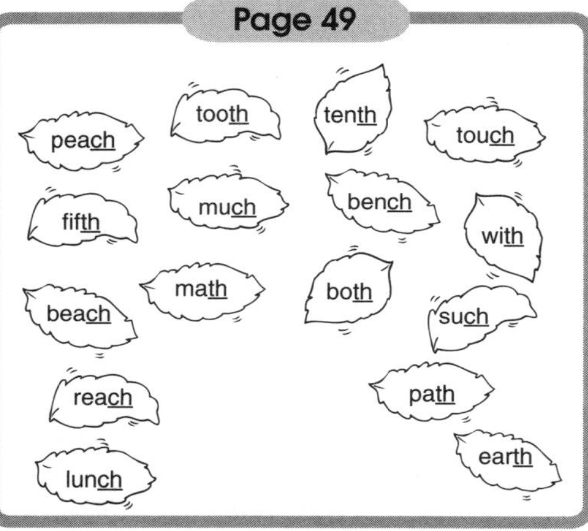

peach
tooth
tenth
touch
fifth
much
bench
with
beach
math
both
such
reach
path
earth
lunch

Page 54

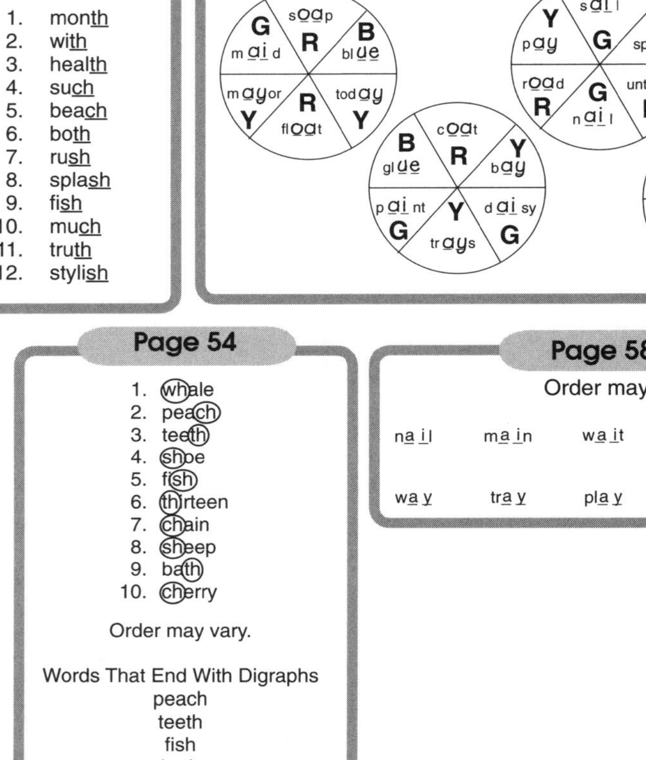

1. whale
2. peach
3. teeth
4. shoe
5. fish
6. thirteen
7. chain
8. sheep
9. bath
10. cherry

Order may vary.

Words That End With Digraphs
peach
teeth
fish
bath

Words That Begin With Digraphs
whale
shoe
thirteen
chain
sheep
cherry

Page 58

Order may vary.

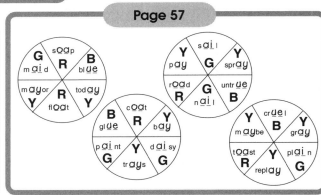

nail	main	wait	aid	tail
way	tray	play	day	say

Page 50

1.	path	6.	health	11.	fish	16.	fresh
2.	flash	7.	north	12.	crash	17.	month
3.	earth	8.	booth	13.	truth	18.	dish
4.	south	9.	both	14.	brush	19.	cash
5.	splash	10.	cloth	15.	push	20.	trash

Page 51

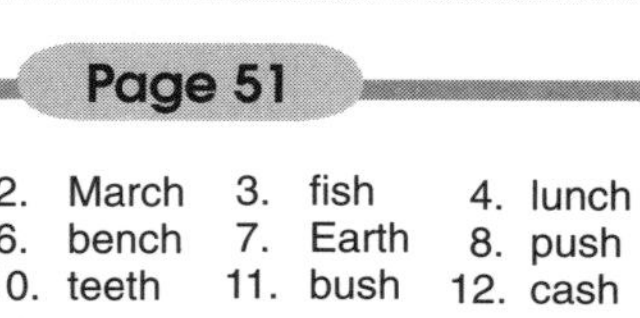

1.	bath	2.	March	3.	fish	4.	lunch
5.	north	6.	bench	7.	Earth	8.	push
9.	trash	10.	teeth	11.	bush	12.	cash

Page 55

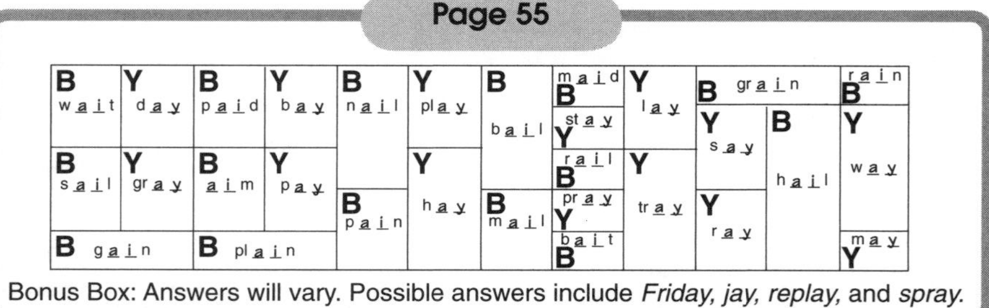

B wait
Y day
B paid
Y bay
B nail
Y play
B bail
B maid
Y stay
Y lay
B grain
B rain
B sail
Y gray
B aim
Y pay
Y hay
B rail
Y pray
Y tray
Y say
B hail
Y way
B gain
B plain
B pain
B mail
B bait
Y ray
Y may

Bonus Box: Answers will vary. Possible answers include *Friday, jay, replay,* and *spray.*

Page 59

cheese G
wheel G
peach Y
ear Y
leaf Y
feet G
steam Y
jeep G
bead Y
queen G
teeth G
tear Y
knee G
tea Y

Page 62

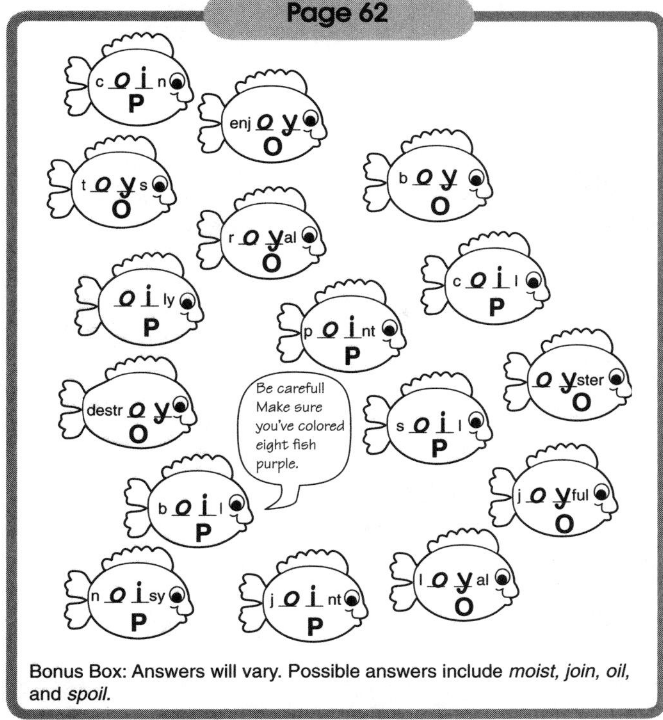

coin P
enjoy O
toys O
boy O
royal O
oily P
coil P
point P
oyster O
destroy O
Be careful! Make sure you've colored eight fish purple.
soil P
boil P
joyful O
noisy P
joint P
loyal O

Bonus Box: Answers will vary. Possible answers include *moist, join, oil,* and *spoil.*

Page 60

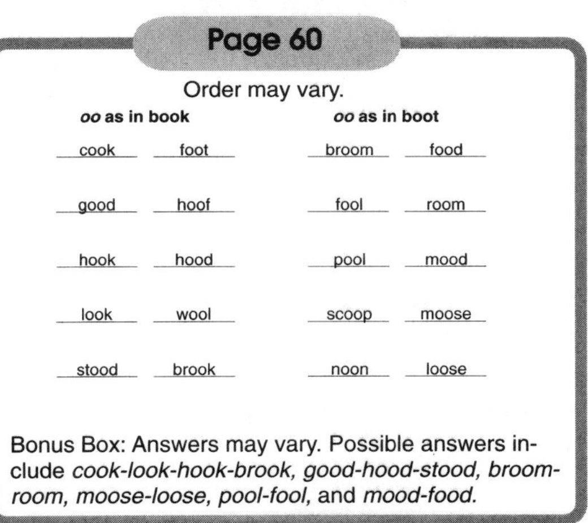

Order may vary.

oo as in book		*oo* as in boot	
cook	foot	broom	food
good	hoof	fool	room
hook	hood	pool	mood
look	wool	scoop	moose
stood	brook	noon	loose

Bonus Box: Answers may vary. Possible answers include *cook-look-hook-brook, good-hood-stood, broom-room, moose-loose, pool-fool,* and *mood-food.*

Page 63

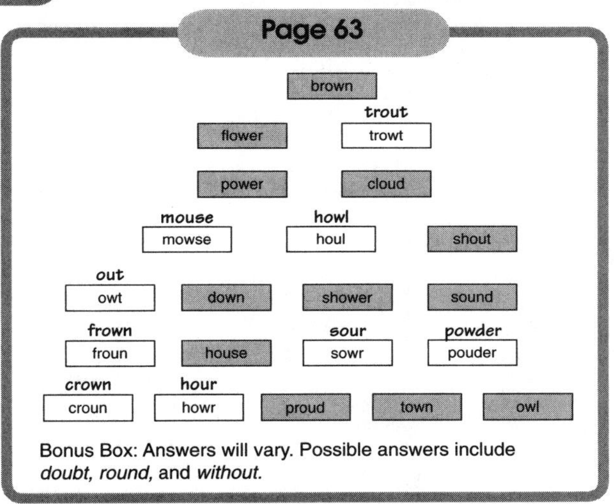

brown
flower
trout
trowt
power
cloud
mouse
mowse
howl
houl
shout
out
owt
down
shower
sound
frown
froun
house
sour
sowr
powder
pouder
crown
croun
hour
howr
proud
town
owl

Bonus Box: Answers will vary. Possible answers include *doubt, round,* and *without.*

Page 61

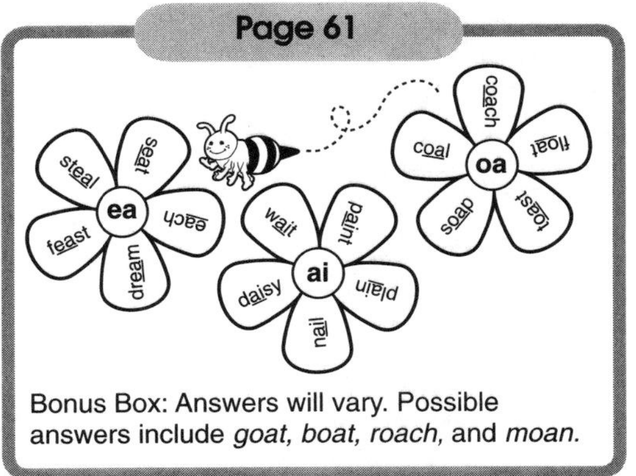

ea
steal
seat
each
dream
feast
ai
wait
paint
plain
nail
daisy
oa
coach
float
toast
soap
coal

Bonus Box: Answers will vary. Possible answers include *goat, boat, roach,* and *moan.*

Page 64

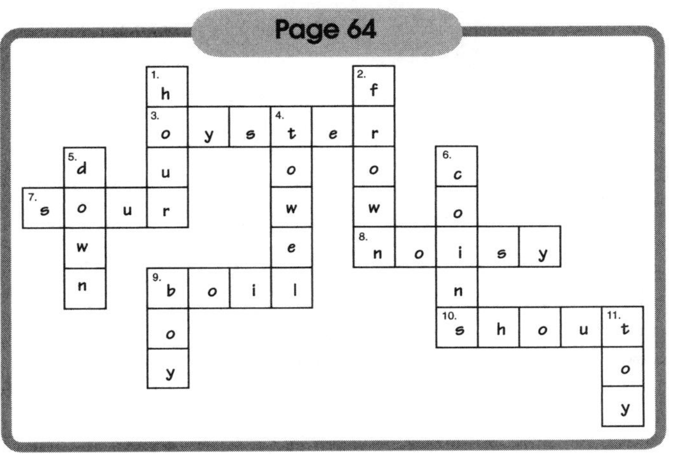

1. hour
2. frown
3. oyster
4. towel
5. down
6. coin
7. sour
8. noisy
9. boil
9. boy
10. shout
11. toy

Page 65

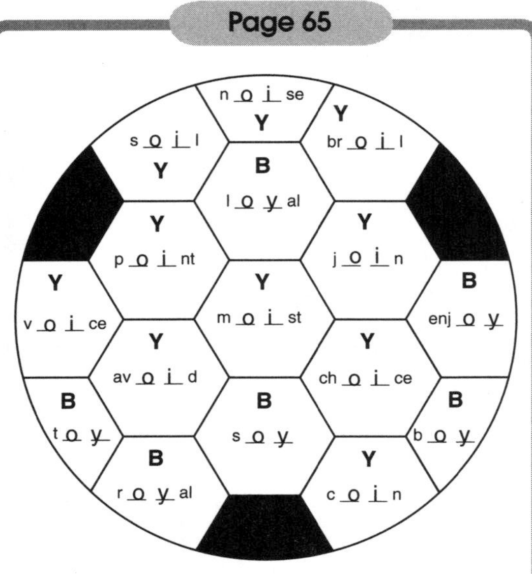

Y noise
Y soil
Y broil
B loyal
Y point
Y join
Y voice
Y moist
B enjoy
Y avoid
Y choice
B toy
B soy
B boy
B royal
Y coin

Bonus Box: Answers will vary. Possible answers include coy, decoy, destroy, employ, Roy, or soy.

Page 69

1. yarn
2. scarf
3. arm
4. horn
5. popcorn
6. storm
7. jar
8. thorn
9. star
10. cart

g	s	h	i	r	t	h	o	r	n
v	c	o	p	o	p	c	o	r	n
r	a	r	m	s	l	a	t	a	l
h	r	n	x	j	a	r	f	s	m
u	f	o	b	y	t	t	e	t	f
n	p	j	r	c	z	d	o	a	w
y	a	r	n	k	s	t	o	r	m

Bonus Box: Answers will vary. Possible answers include *morning, lord, born, cork,* and *fort.*

Page 66

Order may vary.

mound house mouth bounce hour scout

crown brown bow power allow down

Page 70

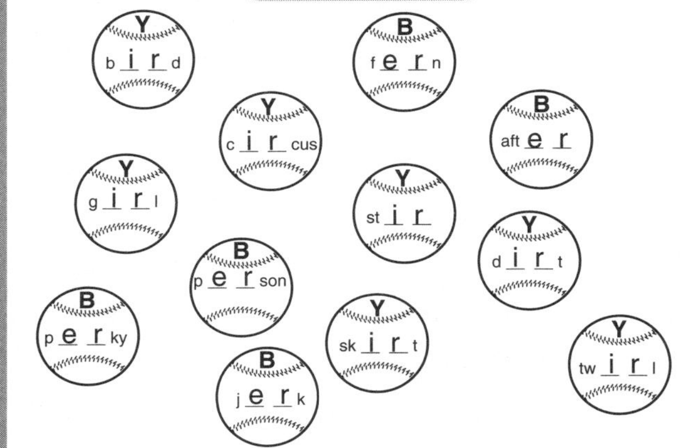

Y bird
B fern
Y circus
B after
Y girl
Y stir
Y dirt
B person
B perky
Y skirt
Y twirl
B jerk

Bonus Box: The student should have circled *mercy* and *thirty.*

Page 67

A	C	R	O	W	N	R
F	L	O	W	E	R	O
M	O	U	T	H	F	U
S	W	L	A	C	O	N
H	N	C	L	O	U	D
O	S	S	K	W	N	O
U	O	U	C	H	D	W
T	O	W	E	L	A	N

Baked ALASKA

1. towel
2. clowns
3. cloud
4. round
5. found
6. down
7. mouth
8. crown
9. shout
10. cow
11. flower
12. ouch

Page 71

jerk turtle termite fur purse

after perch purple hurt hurry

Bonus Box: Answers will vary. Possible answers include *churn, burn, blur,* and *turn.*

Page 72

1. e
2. y
3. f
4. s
5. v
6. t
7. n
8. i
9. r
10. a

Because there's a fan in every seat!

Page 73

1. smart fern perfect
2. certain farmer letter
3. barn party herself
4. garden germs march
5. nerve stern chart
6. summer argue harmful

Bonus Box: Answers will vary.

Page 68

Order of answers may vary.

oi		ow	
soil	coin	powder	growl
noise	moist	crown	shower
voice	point	town	how

Bonus Box: Answers will vary. Possible answers include *cow, flower, wow,* and *tower.*

Page 74

1. the opposite of boy g i r l
2. the center of an apple c o r e
3. the prickly part of a rose t h o r n
4. a make-believe horse with one horn u n i c o r n
5. a bird's sound c h i r p
6. a round shape c i r c l e
7. not clean d i r t y
8. to mix with a spoon s t i r
9. the opposite of less m o r e
10. not exciting b o r i n g

He comes from a whole family of

l o n g (6 10 3 1) J u m p e r s (4 9 5 2 7 8) !

Bonus Box: Answers will vary but may include four of the following words: bird, circus, first, shirt, skirt, born, corn, ford, porch, sport

Page 75

1. start
2. birds
3. cord
4. dark
5. serve
6. forth
7. winter
8. store
9. third
10. first
11. person
12. cards
13. forest
14. yard
15. circus
16. shirt
17. artist
18. cover
19. short
20. perfect

Bonus Box: The student should have written ten list words in alphabetical order.

Page 79

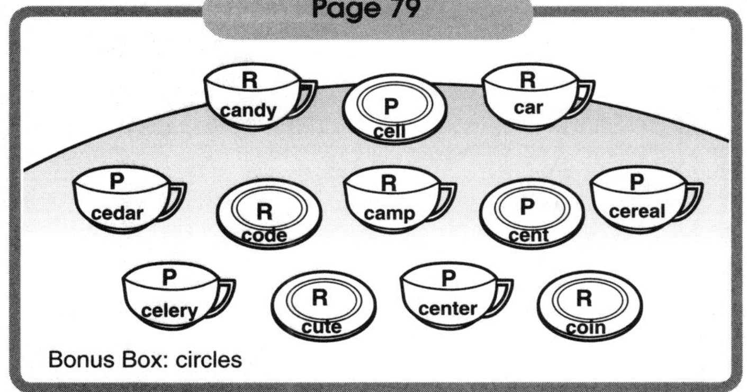

R candy
P cell
R car
P cedar
R code
R camp
P cent
P cereal
P celery
R cute
P center
R coin

Bonus Box: circles

Page 76

1. "Running in Circles"
2. "I've Come So Far to Be a Star"
3. "Birds in the Garden"
4. "Time to Start the Party"
5. "The Third Monday in March"
6. "Stir Things Up, Sir!"
7. "Girl With a Polka-Dot Skirt"
8. "It's Dark at the Market Tonight"
9. "Hard to Always Go First"
10. "Thirty Dirty Pairs of Shoes"

Bonus Box:

1. yellow
2. red
3. orange
4. red
5. orange
6. yellow
7. yellow
8. red
9. orange
10. yellow

Page 80

Order of words within each answer may vary.

scr		thr		wr	
scrabble	scrap	throw	thread	wrinkle	wrapper
scratch	screen	thrifty	thrill	wrestle	wreath

Page 81

1. peach
2. truck
3. watch
4. deck
5. each
6. notch
7. trick
8. stretch
9. which
10. touch
11. fetch
12. clock

Bonus Box: We go to the beach and walk on the dock. Then we eat crunchy snacks while we watch the swimmers.

Page 82

1. yellow, patch
2. green, inch
3. green, much
4. green, pinch
5. yellow, watch
6. green, which
7. green, such
8. yellow, switch
9. green, touch
10. green, reach
11. yellow, itch
12. green, spinach

Page 77

Concirt Review
by G. Girbil

If you haven't seen the Traveling Trio, you're missing a real treat! Hirman, Howie, and Hurbie Hamstir are turrific! Last night, they pirformed in New Jursey. Evury pirson who saw them was thrilled. If you want to see a purfect show, buy a ticket! I'm cirtain you'll love it.

Order may vary.

Concert	Hamster	Every
Gerbil	terrific	person
Herman	performed	perfect
Herbie	Jersey	certain

Page 83

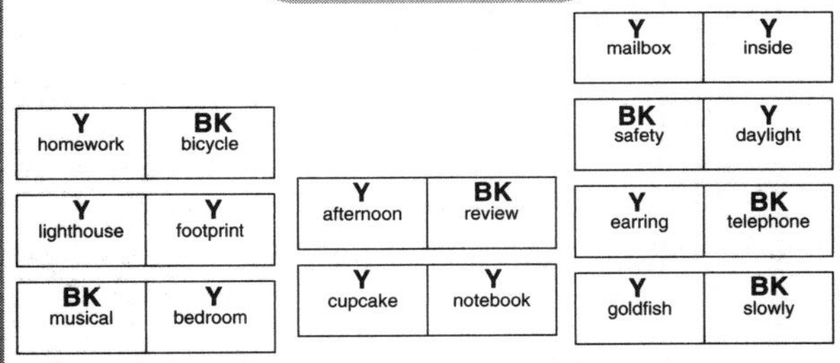

Y mailbox
Y inside
BK safety
Y daylight
Y homework
BK bicycle
Y afternoon
BK review
Y earring
BK telephone
Y lighthouse
Y footprint
Y cupcake
Y notebook
Y goldfish
BK slowly
BK musical
Y bedroom

Bonus Box: Answers will vary. Possible answers include *somebody, someday, somehow, sometime, somewhat,* and *somewhere.*

Page 78

Order of answers on each cookie sheet may vary.

gym giant gum golf

gem gain

gentle gypsy gobble gave

Page 84

1. paintbrush
2. watermelon
3. doorbell
4. rattlesnake
5. anywhere
6. seesaw
7. beehive
8. teamwork
9. earthquake
10. understand

Page 85

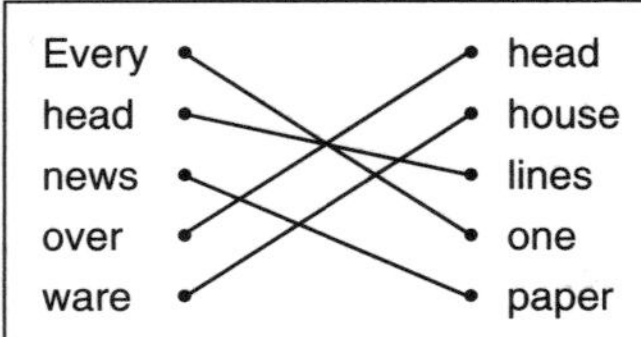

Every
head
news
over
ware
head
house
lines
one
paper

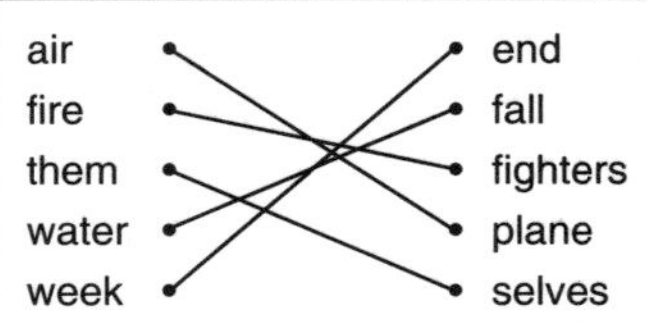

air
fire
them
water
week
end
fall
fighters
plane
selves

Pick up a newspaper! Read the headlines! Last weekend, there was a big fire. An empty warehouse was burning. The firefighters were the first to arrive. They could not put out the fire by themselves. Then they saw something flying overhead! It wasn't an airplane. It was an elephant! He sprayed a waterfall from his trunk. Everyone agrees that this elephant is a hero!

Page 88

Mia Mole's favorite **video** (R) game is "Underground Adventure." **She's** (Y) a very good player, but she **doesn't** (Y) like to play alone. She often **asks** (R) her brother Marco to join her. Then **he'll** (Y) play too. Mia and Marco **want** (R) to win the game. **They'll** (Y) travel through the **tunnels** (R) together. They **won't** (Y) stop until they succeed. Mia is best at digging holes. And Marco? **He's** (Y) a great treasure finder! **It's** (Y) **lots** (R) of fun for them to play together. **They're** (Y) a great team!

1. She's = She + is
2. doesn't = does + not
3. he'll = he + will
4. They'll = They + will
5. won't = will + not
6. He's = He + is
7. It's = It + is
8. They're = They + are

Bonus Box: Answers will vary.

Page 92

	add -s	add -es
1. box	O	(R)
2. rabbit	(C)	H
3. hat	(A)	S
4. glass	T	(D)
5. cape	(O)	A
6. fox	B	(A)
7. kiss	C	(B)
8. wand	(R)	H

"ABRADA-COBRA!"

Bonus Box: boxes, rabbits, hats, glasses, capes, foxes, kisses, wands

Page 93

1. problems
2. bunches
3. things
4. watches
5. patches
6. tricks
7. bushes
8. hats
9. wishes
10. wands

Page 86

1. oatmeal
2. birdhouse
3. weekend
4. nutcracker
5. underground
6. themselves
7. pancake
8. footprints

1. underground
2. footprints
3. oatmeal
4. weekend

Page 89

Order of answers may vary.

I'll	she'll	don't	you've
he'll	I've	they're	haven't
it'll	won't	they've	doesn't
they'll	he's	aren't	she's
you'll	isn't	you're	it's

Page 94

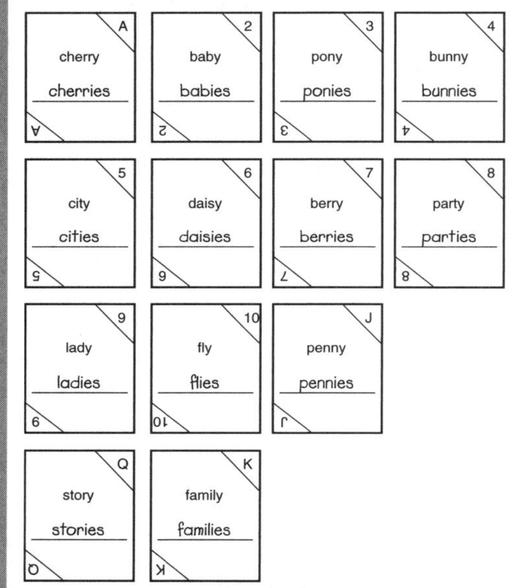

A cherry cherries
2 baby babies
3 pony ponies
4 bunny bunnies
5 city cities
6 daisy daisies
7 berry berries
8 party parties
9 lady ladies
10 fly flies
J penny pennies
Q story stories
K family families

Page 87

Order may vary.

1. bluebirds
2. butterflies
3. grasshopper
4. inchworm
5. maybe
6. raindrops
7. outside
8. springtime
9. sunflowers
10. treetops

In the Backyard

Look closely and maybe you will see
A small inchworm or a buzzing bee.
Feathery bluebirds sing songs for hours,
And tiny seeds become sunflowers.
Green leaves appear on high treetops,
And gray clouds send down small raindrops.
A grasshopper might go jumping by,
Or butterflies may glide through the sky.
Yes, springtime days are filled with fun
And playing outside in the warm, bright sun.

Bonus Box: Answers may vary. Possible answers include *ladybug, dragonfly,* and *firefly.*

Page 90

you'll
I'm
aren't
we're
YOU
they've
won't
it's
he'd
WIN!
I've
she's
didn't
they're

Page 91

1. we will
2. he is
3. I am
4. do not
5. we are
6. is not
7. are not
8. I will
9. they are
10. you have
11. it is
12. can not
13. they have
14. will not

Bonus Box: Answers may vary. Possible answers include *wouldn't, couldn't, didn't,* and *haven't.*

Page 95

1. geese
2. oxen
3. sheep
4. cacti
5. teeth
6. women
7. mice
8. feet
9. deer
10. children

please and thank you

Page 96

Order of answers on each bag may vary.

Add -s	Add -es
shirts	toothbrushes
pencils	lunches
folders	pencil boxes
notebooks	watches
socks	glasses
rulers	
markers	

Page 97

Y
flowers
B
boxes
G
babies
G
families
Y
bees
B
classes
G
parties
B
lunches

1. flowers
2. Bees
3. Families or Classes

Page 98

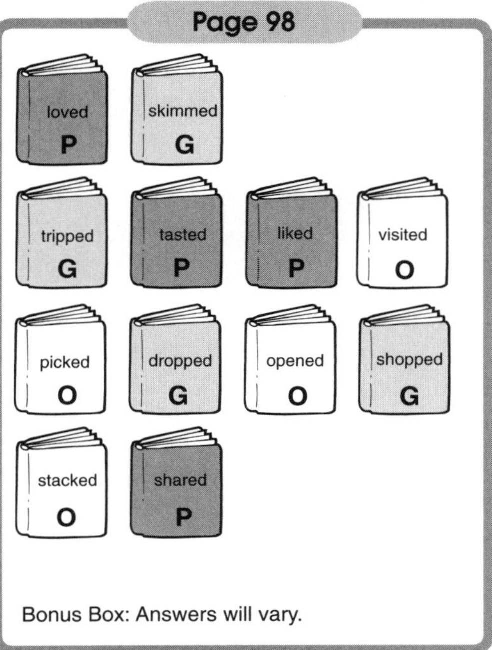
loved
P
skimmed
G
tripped
G
tasted
P
liked
P
visited
O
picked
O
dropped
G
opened
O
shopped
G
stacked
O
shared
P

Bonus Box: Answers will vary.

Page 99

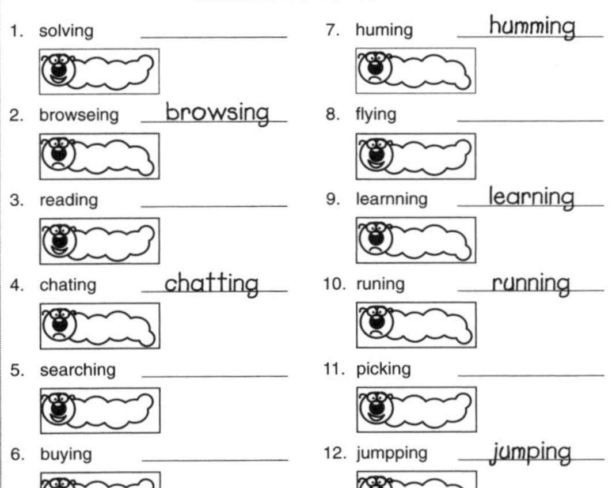

1. solving
2. browseing — browsing
3. reading
4. chating — chatting
5. searching
6. buying
7. huming — humming
8. flying
9. learnning — learning
10. runing — running
11. picking
12. jumpping — jumping

Page 100

1. Batting
2. Saved
3. Played
4. Bathing
5. Caged
6. Visiting
7. Soaring
8. Learned
9. Tracking
10. Cheered
11. Racing
12. Missed

Bonus Box: Answers will vary.

Page 101

1. clucked clucking
2. gobbled gobbling
3. soared soaring
4. perched perching
5. pecked pecking
6. hopped hopping
7. nested nesting
8. swooped swooping
9. glided gliding
10. waddled waddling

Bonus Box: Students should have colored the books with the following words: *cluck, soar, perch, peck, nest,* and *swoop.*

Page 102

1. wanted **B**
2. liked **P**
3. skimmed **G**
4. switched **B**
5. planned **G**
6. decided **P**
7. laughed **B**
8. loved **P**

Bonus Box: The student should have written a sentence that includes the word *shopped.*

Page 103

1. It's an ________ day for Sandy and Shelly.
   (exciting) exciteing excited
2. They're ________ surfing!
   gooing goed (going)
3. They start ________ to the water.
   runing runned (running)
4. Sandy starts ________.
   paddleing (paddling) paddled
5. Shelly begins ________ her feet.
   (kicking) kickking kicked
6. The friends are ________ through the water.
   (racing) raccing raceing
7. They sit ________ for a big wave.
   waitting waited (waiting)
8. Then they see it ________!
   comming (coming) comeing
9. ________ up, they catch the wave!
   Jumpping (Jumping) Jump
10. They are a pair of ________ seals!
    (surfing) surffing surfeing

Page 104

1. cried
2. jogged
3. carried
4. diving
5. talked
6. swimming
7. smiled
8. hopped
9. surfing
10. wanted
11. taking
12. moving
13. washed
14. laughing
15. tried
16. running
17. waved
18. planting
19. hurried
20. giving

Page 105

1. June enjoy s picnics!
2. This morning, she ask ed Wally whether he wanted to go.
3. Wally couldn't wait to get start ed.
4. June began pack ing a basket full of food.
5. Wally love s to eat fruit.
6. The friends started look ing for a perfect spot.
7. June like s to sit under the trees.
8. The friends sat and began eat ing their fruit.
9. Wally always count s the seeds in his piece.
10. When it started to get dark, June and Wally head ed home.

Page 106

1. unclean
2. unsafe
3. unclog
4. repaint
5. replaced
6. refilled
7. renew
8. reappeared
9. unusual
10. uncool

Page 107

1. B
2. G
3. F
4. L
5. D
6. J
7. H
8. I
9. C
10. A
11. K
12. E

Page 108

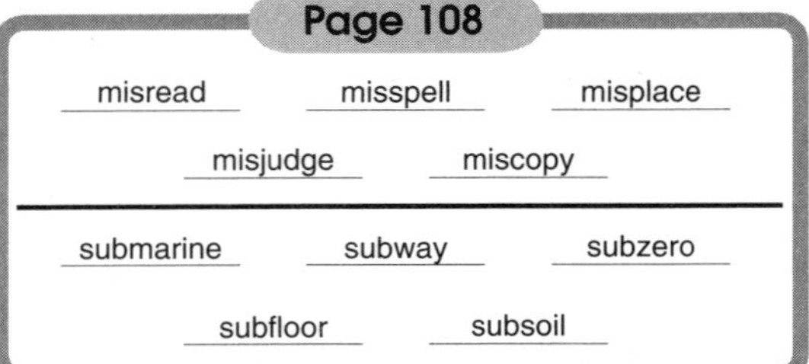

misread
misspell
misplace
misjudge
miscopy
submarine
subway
subzero
subfloor
subsoil

Page 109

1. wider
2. duller
3. softest
4. thinner
5. thickest
6. fastest
7. darker
8. strongest
9. sharpest
10. cheaper

Page 110

1. faithful
2. helpless
3. thankful
4. flawless
5. effortless
6. thoughtful
7. colorful
8. priceless

Bonus Box: Answers will vary.

Page 111

Order of answers in each set may vary.

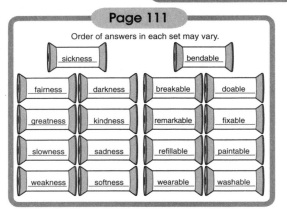

sickness
fairness
darkness
greatness
kindness
slowness
sadness
weakness
softness

bendable
breakable
doable
remarkable
fixable
refillable
paintable
wearable
washable

Page 112

1. passable
2. prideful
3. fixable
4. thankful
5. useful
6. stretchable
7. hopeful
8. powerful
9. washable
10. truthful

u	l	v	d	g	y	b	i	f	r	o	h	p	r	i	d	e	f	u	l	f	x	o
s	t	r	e	t	c	h	a	b	l	e	o	c	i	v	o	g	h	p	k	i	r	v
e	d	c	l	b	z	a	h	i	s	q	p	w	a	s	h	a	b	l	e	x	l	n
f	z	s	b	r	c	a	y	u	g	r	e	p	m	h	u	l	p	i	w	a	y	h
u	m	p	o	w	e	r	f	u	l	j	f	n	j	b	p	a	s	s	a	b	l	e
l	e	m	k	t	d	t	f	x	u	p	u	k	t	r	u	t	h	f	u	l	j	a
e	t	f	n	t	h	a	n	k	f	u	l	f	w	a	d	k	q	e	q	e	m	w

Page 113

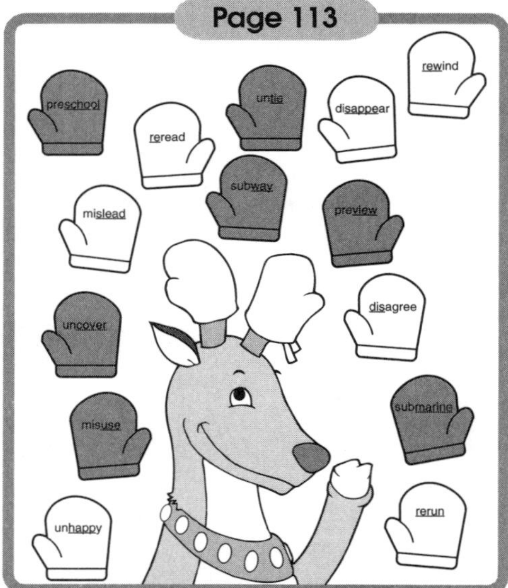

rewind
preschool
untie
disappear
reread
subway
mislead
preview
disagree
uncover
submarine
misuse
unhappy
rerun

Page 114

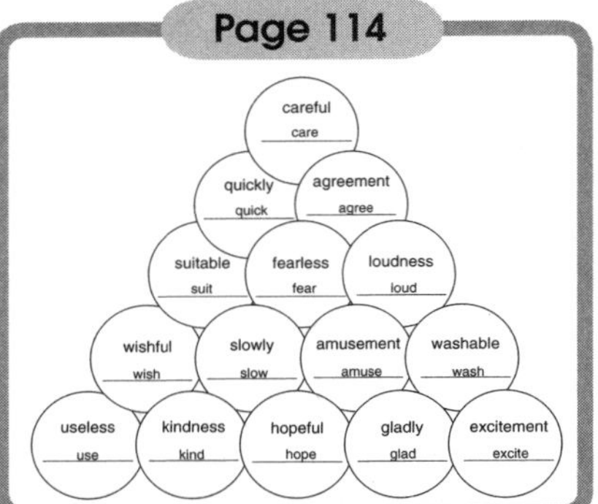

careful
care
quickly
quick
agreement
agree
suitable
suit
fearless
fear
loudness
loud
wishful
wish
slowly
slow
amusement
amuse
washable
wash
useless
use
kindness
kind
hopeful
hope
gladly
glad
excitement
excite

Page 115

Word Bank

joyful
preheat
enjoyable
retry
coldness
endless
replay
quickly
sleepless
wishful
lovely
rebuild

1. play
2. enjoy
3. quick
4. try
5. end
6. love
7. build
8. cold
9. joy
10. wish
11. heat
12. sleep

Bonus Box: Answers will vary.

Page 116

1. went
2. flew
3. rode
4. took
5. ran
6. friends
7. slid
8. thought

Bonus Box: The student should have circled *because* and *find.*

Page 117

Three ladybug ~~freinds~~ friends met at the park. They stood on the ~~playgrownd~~ playground and looked around. There ~~where~~ were so many things to do! ~~Thay~~ They chose to go on the swings ~~furst.~~ first. Each ladybug sat on a swing and swung ~~hi~~ high in the air. It felt ~~grate~~ great to go so high! They talked and sang together. Then they rode ~~thee~~ the merry-go-round. They spun around ~~untill~~ until they were dizzy. ~~Wat~~ What a fun day for the three spotted friends!

Page 118

Order of answers may vary.

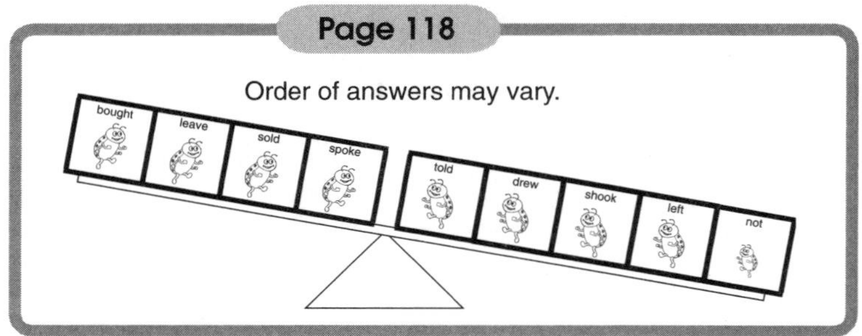

bought
leave
sold
spoke
told
drew
shook
left
not